HAPPILY EVER
ESTHER

HAPPILY EVER ESTHER

TWO MEN, A WONDER PIG, AND THEIR LIFE-CHANGING
MISSION TO GIVE ANIMALS A HOME

STEVE JENKINS, DEREK WALTER,
AND CAPRICE CRANE

GRAND CENTRAL
PUBLISHING

NEW YORK   BOSTON

Grand Central Publishing
Hachette Book Group
1290 Avenue of the Americas, New York, NY 10104
grandcentralpublishing.com
twitter.com/grandcentralpub

First Edition: July 2018

Grand Central Publishing is a division of Hachette Book Group, Inc. The Grand Central Publishing name and logo is a trademark of Hachette Book Group, Inc.

The publisher is not responsible for websites (or their content) that are not owned by the publisher.

The Hachette Speakers Bureau provides a wide range of authors for speaking events. To find out more, go to www.hachettespeakersbureau.com or call (866) 376-6591.

Unless noted, all photos courtesy of the authors.

Library of Congress Cataloging-in-Publication Data

Names: Jenkins, Steve, 1982- author. | Walter, Derek, 1981- author.
Title: Happily Ever Esther / Steve Jenkins, Derek Walter, and Caprice Crane.
Description: First edition. | New York : Grand Central Publishing, 2018.
Identifiers: LCCN 2017046608 | ISBN 9781538728147 (hardcover) |
    ISBN 9781549169120 (audio download) | ISBN 9781538728123 (ebook)
Subjects: LCSH: Swine as pets—Canada—Anecdotes. | Animal sanctuaries—
    Canada—Anecdotes. | Domestic animals—Care—Canada—Anecdotes. | Farm
    life—Canada—Anecdotes. | Human-animal relationships.
Classification: LCC SF395.6 .J47 2018 | DDC 636.4/0887—dc23
LC record available at https://lccn.loc.gov/2017046608

ISBNs: 978-1-5387-2814-7 (hardcover), 978-1-5387-2812-3 (ebook), 978-1-5387-3194-9 (signed edition), 978-1-5387-3193-2 (B&N signed edition)

Printed in the United States of America

LSC-C

10 9 8 7 6 5 4 3 2 1

To Esther. For inspiring us in a way we never imagined. For making us laugh, smile, and want to be better people. You represent everything good in this world, and we'll forever be thankful for the day you came storming into our lives.

To all the people who have embraced an Esther-Approved lifestyle, you can do it. The world is becoming a kinder place every day because of people like you.

And to the millions of Esthers around the world that haven't been so lucky. Slowly but surely the world is waking up; we're just sorry it's taking so long.

FOREWORD

It may seem strange to equate a 650-pound pig with a butterfly, but when the pig in question is Esther, I believe the comparison is valid.

Just as chaos theory shows us that the flapping of butterfly wings can cause ripples of change to emanate across our universe and truly alter the path of our lives, so too have those of us who have been drawn into Esther's spell had our horizons expanded, our preconceptions challenged, and our hearts swollen.

It is not hyperbole to call Esther a phenomenon. She is a truly magical creature, not only in terms of the lives she has touched and the awareness she has raised, but most of all—and this is surely the root of all her other powers—she is just such a beautiful spirit to hang out with.

Like many of her disciples, I became enamored with her initially via her social media presence, and my fascination with her only increased when I made the pilgrimage to the

Happily Ever Esther Farm Sanctuary and was granted an audience with the Princess of Porcine.

Of course, the two people whose lives have been most altered by Esther's magic are her dads, Steve Jenkins and Derek Walter. To say their lives were turned upside down when they adopted what they thought was a teacup piglet would be insulting to understatements. They are now living on and running a farm animal sanctuary and managing a veritable Esther empire that includes merchandise, social media, cruises, and activism for a variety of animal and social causes.

This book picks up where their last left off, and details the realities of suddenly finding themselves living in a freezing farmhouse and in charge of a farm that is rapidly filling up with rescue animals. To say they learn on the job is also an understatement, but what keeps them going is their love for a pig and the way she inspires them and so many other people to make the world a better, kinder place—even when she (spoiler alert) goes through her awkward teenager phase and won't speak to them for days on end!

This book is a lesson in resilience, grace, and love. The day I spent hanging out with Esther, Steve, and Derek (not forgetting Cornelius the turkey and Reuben and Shelby the dogs) was one of the fondest of my life. This book re-illuminated and reminded me of what it feels like to be a part of the Esther experience in all its shapes and forms, in all its joy and pain, in all its huge implications for how we can change the world, and in all its tiniest moments of purity, such as when you look Esther in the eye and you feel happy she is alive and you have been a part of her life.

—Alan Cumming
January 2018

HAPPILY EVER
ESTHER

PROLOGUE

Bringing home a new family member can be a life-altering experience. It's something that should never be taken lightly. It usually happens only after months, sometimes even years, of research and planning. At least it does for any sensible person—something I, Steve, have never claimed to be.

Animals have a way of finding me. Like our dog Shelby, whom we were just supposed to be babysitting, but then her family moved away and never came back. Or our cat Delores, who was the runt in a litter of barn cats a girlfriend brought to my attention. I went to feed the cats once and came home with Delores because the others wouldn't let her eat.

Yes, it's a pattern.

So when I got a message about a mini-pig that needed a home, there was only one thing I could do: say yes! Thankfully, my amazing partner, Derek, is never one to shy away from an adventure. But little did we know this was going to be unlike any adventure we had ever been on. Our sweet, tiny, five-pound mini-pig grew up to be a 650-pound, full-sized commercial pig.

Finding out the truth about who Esther was caused us to completely reevaluate who we were and how we lived our lives. Learning to live with a 650-pound pig in our 1,000-square-foot home nearly drove us to our breaking point. There were sleepless nights, heated conversations, and many, many tears. But we soldiered on and challenged ourselves in ways we had never dreamed of before.

We thought we had been through the worst until we started an Esther the Wonder Pig Facebook page that would take things to a whole new level of crazy. Within weeks her page went viral, amassing over one hundred thousand likes in under eighty days. Unfortunately, we lived in a town whose bylaws prohibited us from keeping Esther. Facing the risk of losing her to town officials, we had a serious decision to make: shut down the page and quietly fade away... or get serious about realizing our new dream of opening a farm sanctuary. We knew we could rescue many more "Esthers," along with other abused and abandoned farm animals that needed a safe-forever home.

Five months after the page began—and less than two years after we met Esther for the very first time—we launched a crowdfunding campaign that raised more than $440,000 to buy the farm in just sixty days.

We had somehow done what everyone told us was impossible. This was our Happily Ever Esther.

CHAPTER ONE

People often think about giving it all up and just moving to a farm. It's an old cliché. *Everything will be wonderful,* they think. And in theory, sure—it sounds great. Waking to the melodious sounds of birds chirping, breathing in fresh air as you sip your morning coffee on the porch and watch the livestock frolic. (Here's where the comedic record scratch would sound, to emphasize how wrong your theory would be.) The realities of actually closing up shop on the life you've always known and moving to a farm—when, by the way, you have never actually been a farmer—are frantic, crazy, and potentially insane.

So, of course, that's what we did.

At first, none of the realities had sunk in quite yet; that would take a few more hours. And then deeper realities about the magnitude of what we'd committed to would sink in over the next few days, weeks, and months. But they couldn't possibly set in yet, because there was still no normalcy. So we were just going with the flow, moment to moment, not even in the same area code of realizing what we had just done.

There we were, being greeted by friends and strangers, in the middle of an extremely surreal situation. I mean, let's be real, how many people move into their new home with a party for them already taking place? That was us. (We rarely do things without some sort of flourish.)

When we first arrived at the farm, we had tons of guests on our property, milling about with wide eyes and big smiles, all there to welcome us to our new home. While we'd never moved to a farm before, we had previously changed homes, and that change had certainly never come with an army of well-wishers.

All the fanfare and excitement made it impossible to really think about anything but what was happening in the moment. And that first moment was all about introducing Esther to her new home: a seemingly immeasurable farm.

But let's pause to set the scene: It was the first time Esther had been on the farm, finally getting her first look at this enormous playground. Esther was no longer our (admittedly poorly kept) secret, hidden away in a suburban home. Now she finally had some room to move, to get her groove on. We just hoped it wasn't too much for her. (Or us.)

While Esther was a bit shell-shocked at first, the comforting presence of Shelby, who helped guide her off the trailer and into her new pasture, seemed to put her at ease. We took Esther on a full-perimeter tour of the pasture, Shelby and our other dog, Reuben, on either side of her. And even though we were surrounded by all those guests, in that moment it felt like it was just us. Our little family of five: Derek, Esther, Shelby, Reuben, and me. (And of course the cats, but they weren't going to tour the farm; they still had their knickers in a twist about the move. Something about the feline disposition doesn't immediately take well to being uprooted.)

I remember searching Esther's face to see if I could read her mind or know what she was thinking. Was she happy? Did she like the pasture? Had we done well? There was definitely a spring in her step and that familiar smile on her face, which comforted me no end. After all, this whole venture was entirely for Esther's sake. We really needed her to like it. And she seemed to, which was a relief.

In a heartfelt if slightly awkward speech, Derek and I thanked everyone for being there. We were truly grateful for the support, but, to be honest, we also wanted the party to be over. I know that sounds terrible; people had come a long way to "see us in." (Is that the correct term? I know when you're going away, people "see you off," but this was the opposite of that.) They'd all traveled from far and wide, and we certainly appreciated it. But there we were, checking our watches and waiting for them to leave. It sounds a bit harsh, but I think anyone in our situation would have felt the same. This whole process was incredibly overwhelming. We had a lot to do. Derek even had to make one last trip back to our former home, in Georgetown, to get the last of our belongings, and he couldn't leave until all these people did.

Granted, this had been our idea. We'd welcomed people to witness our first day really taking over the farm, particularly Esther's first steps at her new home. But if you've ever made a big move, you know how physically and emotionally exhausting it can be, and that feeling was (at least) tripled for us. We needed time to ourselves, to get centered, to get our plans together and figure out what we'd gotten ourselves into.

By the time it was just us again, it quickly became just me. Derek was en route to Georgetown, and I was at the farm virtually alone. When we moved from Georgetown, we planned to let Esther decide whether she'd continue to sleep in the house or become a barn pig, and Esther had made her decision clear: she and the dogs had fallen asleep in the house. So I was free to explore the new place entirely by myself. It was a very rare moment of total solitude, and it was amazing. I had time to really take in the day and (of course) overwhelm myself with my own thoughts. Things got more and more frightening as I let my mind wander, so I poured myself a glass of wine and took a few deep breaths, trying to remain calm and visualize what this new life would be.

I walked out to the barn and around the silo. After a while of fantasizing, I realized it hardly seemed fair for me to just be relaxing at the farm while Derek was working like crazy at the Georgetown house. So I went back into the house and tried to put some boxes away. It was the least I could do.

When Derek returned, he somehow found the energy to unload the rest of our stuff from the truck. We put our mattress in the sunroom and tried to move the boxes to the locations where we'd be unpacking them, to make life easier. (You know the feeling on the back end of a big move: you just want to drop every box in the closest open space. Tempting, sure, but it just makes things much more challenging later on.)

By the time we finished moving the last box, Esther was already on the mattress, happily snoring away. Can't say we were surprised.

It was tough winding down from such an excitement-filled day. We didn't have TV or internet service yet. It was just us, our dogs, and our cell phones on the couch, a pig in our bed. Our property had come with a mobile home where the daughter of the previous owner had lived with her husband, and we had put the cats in there for the day, because we knew people would be going in and out of the house, moving in the boxes and furniture, and the doors would be constantly open. We figured it would be safer to tuck the cats over there, so they could at least be out of their travel crates and explore the mobile home. When we finally decided to go to sleep, I wound up sharing the bed with Esther, while Derek slept on the couch.

Waking up the next morning was surreal. For starters, I was in a sunroom on a mattress with a pig. But it was my first morning in these new surroundings, and I was startled when I opened my eyes. It took me a minute to regroup and remember: *Oh yeah, we bought a farm. We live here now. There's Derek with one leg hanging off the couch. This is our new life.*

When we woke Esther up, we already had breakfast (pig kibble and fresh produce) waiting for her in the kitchen. Once Esther was satiated, the three of us went for a walk. It was our first walk as a family without crowds of well-wishers watching Esther's every move, and she had a real jump in her step. We didn't go too far, but enough to let Esther wander. It was all so new, and she wanted to dig up everything in sight. We let her go places we hadn't gone the day before, such as into the field and into the forest. That's where she was really excited to dig. It was pretty special just watching her explore, imagining all the things we'd do and build. The future.

But the fantasizing was short-lived. We brought the cats into the house, and they were skittish. We'd see a blur of orange every now and then as a cat ran past. They might have thought we were going to catch them and take them away again. They were exploring every nook and cranny of the house, but the minute you walked into the room they'd duck and run for cover. It took them awhile to realize this was their new home and everything was okay. Our dogs get separation anxiety, so they stuck by us at all times for the first week.

Also, the work had to start. There's so much to do when you move to a new space—especially one that's been unloved for such a long time, as our new home had been. The barn was filthy and needed to be addressed, but the most pressing issue was that the farm had no adequate fencing. There was an existing electric fence, but it didn't work. We knew we would be getting a horse and a donkey soon, and we had to have fences in place by then.

This was all new to me. I'd never built a fence before, let alone an electric one, but Derek seemed to understand what was going on. We made a Hail Mary plea to a couple of friends to help us, and with their assistance we replaced the existing electric fence with new and working materials. Luckily, the property had come with a couple of rolls of heavy-gauge wire, which got us started. We had to use T-bars to mount the fence, because we didn't have time to get wood posts into the ground. The sellers had also told us that digging would be difficult because of all the rock. So using the metal T-bars was the quickest and easiest way to get something up rapidly.

I know the idea of an electric fence might sound cruel at first, but it doesn't hurt when you get shocked. Believe me: I've tried it. Imagine one of those gag-buzzers that you get as a toy to zap someone. It's just surprising, not painful. It scares you, but it doesn't hurt. I'd never put my animal family through anything I wouldn't do myself. We'd truly never do anything that might hurt one of our animals. And they learn really quickly; after they're zapped once, they don't try their luck again. The fence exists for their protection, to keep them from wandering off to somewhere dangerous. I'm thrilled that we found a process that worked well and was, and is still, completely safe for everyone.

The barn was a disaster. We had known that going in, but knowing it doesn't make you feel any better when you consider the work ahead of you. We would have more animals arriving soon, and we had to get the barn ready right away. So the fence and the barn were our top priorities—our house would wait.

There were spiderwebs in the barn that were so thick you could jump on them and they'd hold you like a net. It looked like a horror movie set. I've never seen anything like it. Taking down those spiderwebs was the stuff of nightmares.

Upstairs in the hayloft, there was a ton of old hay with burrowed tunnels through it. We didn't know what lived in there. Raccoons? Possums? The ghosts of farmers past? So we were slowly and carefully rooting through that, unsure of what or whom we might find. We fully expected that a raccoon might jump out and latch onto our faces, but all we found was a big pile of poo. This all had to go, so we could get fresh hay ready for the animals.

Oh, and you know how we mentioned we had a horse and a donkey arriving soon and thus the need for the fence? Now, we were also expecting four new pigs and needed a place to secure them—and fast. We were literally twisting the last piece of wiring on their fence as the trailer transporting the new arrivals (Bobbie, Dan, Leonard, and Bear) pulled into the driveway.

But let's back up. How did we go from a horse and a donkey to four more huge commercial pigs in the time we were still building a fence? Good question. We're glad you asked it—or, at least, we're going to pretend you did.

We'd been contacted by a woman named Mary who ran a rescue organization in Ontario. Mary was friendly with a lady named Tara, who ran a sanctuary on the border of Quebec. Tara's sanctuary apparently had fallen on hard times, mostly because Tara was in her late seventies, and she was having trouble managing it all. She might have had a smoothly running operation at some point, but she'd been doing this for thirty years, her husband had passed away, and she was now totally on her own. She didn't have regular help or any kind of volunteer base.

Tara, however, wasn't ready to admit it was time to hang it up. It was other people in the rescue world who were complaining to animal control about her, which rang alarm bells for Mary. If animal control got involved, Tara's animals would either go to market or be killed. So Mary was desperate to find a new home for four pigs and three cows. (Oh, right. We'd also be getting three cows. This is apparently how things go.)

Mary found us online, as most people do, and sent us an email via our website. At the time, our website was still directly connected to my phone, so I got her email right away. If that email came in today, we'd go through a series of questions first: Is it a farmed animal? Whom else have you spoken to? Are we the last resort? Is there anything we can do to fix the situation so the owners don't have to get rid of the animal? If after that, all answers still seem to point to us, the decision then goes to the board. They have to give their final blessing before we agree to take the animal.

(A brief aside: I'm on the board, so I get a say, but ultimately Krista and Susan can outvote me anytime.) We've known Susan for years, and she's married to another good friend of ours named Ray, whom I first met when we started working in real estate together. Susan is a businesswoman in her own right, and she had spent a ton of time volunteering for various organizations and sat on other boards. This would be her first farm sanctuary, but she had all kinds of experience that Derek and I didn't. That's the kind of person we knew we needed to surround ourselves with, so Susan was a natural choice. Krista had come into our lives only after Esther burst onto the scene in 2014. She works for Mercy for Animals, one of the largest animal rights organizations in the world. She's got a larger-than-life personality, and she's ridiculously knowledgeable in all things animal rights. We quickly became great friends with Krista and her husband, Nigel, so she too was a natural choice when it came time to create our own board of directors.

But back then, during the Tara situation, we hadn't put any processes in place. So I emailed back and said we could talk about it. After a few exchanges, I said, "Okay, we'll make it work." I'd never even met a cow before, so I was excited about that. Of course, we weren't settled or organized, and we weren't equipped for more animals. But we had a farm, and dammit, I wanted to take the animals.

As soon as people got wind that we were taking these new animals—this is a very gossipy business, and word gets around fast—people started sending us messages about how terrible they believed this Tara person to be. It was upsetting, to say the least. We weren't hearing from a bunch of people rallying to support this poor woman who had dedicated her life to helping animals—they were attacking her behind her back, and it struck us as really mean.

At some point Derek and I will need to retire, and I know running a sanctuary is a double-edged sword. For now, I love helping animals so much, I can't imagine wanting to stop. But there are days when Derek and I are exhausted. I do want to walk away at some point and know that we have a retirement fund, and I hope we can do that while we're still young enough to enjoy it.

Presumably, this woman didn't consider or plan for her retirement. She'd just kept on trucking along until she couldn't anymore. People who run animal sanctuaries can forget that at some point they're not going to be able to do all the things they need to do. It's all fine and good to dedicate your life to saving animals, but everybody needs an exit plan. And if they don't have one, they just become part of the problem they dedicated their life to fixing. All of a sudden there are dozens, sometimes hundreds, of animals that need a home urgently, all because the sanctuary where they live is closing unexpectedly. It can happen for any number of reasons. Sometimes it's poor financial planning, underestimating the costs involved. Or it can be an inability to do the labor required to maintain the farm and its residents. Or sometimes the caregiver/owner passes away, leaving an unwilling family member to take over.

When these things happen, remaining sanctuaries are often called upon to step in and take the animals, but sometimes that's not possible without putting their own farms in financial peril. It's a vicious cycle, and, sadly, not every displaced sanctuary animal finds a new home. Sometimes they end up back where they came from, at an auction on their way to market.

Derek and I are unwilling to let ours become one of those sanctuaries, so we began putting the pieces of our eventual "Departure Plan" in place the minute we arrived on the farm. We hope it'll be decades before it needs to be put into action, but it's really nice to know there are plans in order in the event something unforeseen ever happens.

So, we understood the strong feelings about the Tara situation, but we weren't going to get caught up in the gossip and bad-mouthing. And we were going to take those animals off her hands.

We used Esther's Army, our web page for activism, to recruit some help. Esther's Army had started out as a page to promote our crowdfunding campaign, but by now we'd morphed it into our home base for a more direct form of activism (to rehome animals, campaign against pig-wrestling events, and so on). We posted about the animals needing rescue and asked if anyone could help transport the pigs. One supporter offered a trailer and then coordinated the pigs' transportation, picking them up from Tara's place and bringing them to our farm. It was a long drive, something like seven hours, which was amazing of the volunteers to do, and it was also hard on the pigs.

We decided to keep Esther in the house during their arrival so she wouldn't see what was going on. She was already a bit out of sorts from our move—she was in a new space and had no idea what was happening or why we were there—so the last thing she needed was to see four interloper pigs on her new turf. Esther's sweet as can be, but all animals (including humans—humans most of all, one might argue) have their territorial moments.

Before the pigs arrived, we took Esther on her walk, fed her, and got as many chores out of the way as we could. That meant cleaning stalls, finishing fences, and doing whatever else we could with the time we had. Having cleaned out the mess of all the old hay that came with the farm, we had bought new hay, and we needed to put it away. We plugged in the hay elevator and were astonished to find that it worked. We managed to get all the hay in place before the pigs arrived.

When the trailer pulled up and we opened the door, all four pigs were scared and hiding at the other end of the trailer. We quickly realized that there was no ramp, and a frightened pig was not going to step down a foot and a half into unknown territory. How do you build a ramp? We weren't quite farmers yet. And we certainly had no ramp-building experience. We were two guys from the city, faking it as we went along. So we "built" a makeshift ramp using a bale of hay, some plywood, and a wood crate (and hoped to God it would work). Seeing the pigs all terrified and huddled as far back as they could go in the trailer, we just felt awful. I loved them already—you fall in love with them the minute you meet them. And you know they've arrived in the best place they could possibly go, but in the moment, they don't know that. They have no idea what the hell is going on.

Once the ramp was set up, we coaxed them out one by one. Bear, the black-and-white pig, was the first to venture forth. He tentatively stepped onto the ramp, one leg, then another, then the back legs. But one of his back legs fell through the plywood! (These are not lightweight animals.) Fortunately, Derek and I were standing on either side of Bear, so we lifted him back up. He'd fallen only about six inches, but to a pig on a ramp in an unknown space, it might as well have been three floors. He briefly got stuck and panicked, but we got him down and soothed his nerves with treats.

Once Bear was out, the rest followed suit. (We'd put down a few more layers of wood in this learn-as-you-go experiment.) Then we just let them walk around and get comfortable. We gave them all treats, then got them into their stalls.

We noticed Bear was having trouble with the back leg, and we felt terrible. Here we thought we'd injured him in the first five minutes!

We later learned that we had misread the situation, but the reality still turned out to be concerning. About two weeks after Bear and his buddies arrived, we noticed he was still sitting outside when the three other pigs had come back in. Obviously, something was wrong. We wanted to close the barn for the night and were trying to force Bear to get up, but he just wouldn't stand. Once he finally did, it was clear he was having a really hard time walking.

The next morning our vet came to see Bear and diagnosed him with what seemed to be a terrible case of arthritis. The vet said, "He's gone lame." It was a failure in the back end, and both legs gave out. We put him on pain meds, but it kept progressing to the point where he wouldn't get up at all. The last time he went down, he (thank goodness) happened to be in the barn. He just lay down and has never gotten up again.

While that might sound sad, he has a TV in his stall (yes,

really), and a masseuse visits him once a week. I know that sounds quirky. It wasn't that we thought, *Oh, we must hire a masseuse for this pig!* It just worked out that way. My mom's neighbor has a daughter who did equine therapy, and she mentioned that maybe she could help the pig. To be honest, it hasn't done anything to help the issue, but who wouldn't want a weekly massage? I know I'd like one! So we keep it up. Derek spends three hours a day with Bear. He's in great spirits. He's got his favorite TV shows. Sedentary life for Bear is still pretty good.

The emergency fencing worked until spring, when the pigs started lifting the entire fence and T-bars right out of the muddy ground. At that point, we realized we'd eventually have to put wood posts into the ground no matter how hard it was to dig. But we weren't there yet. We'd just gotten the new pigs settled, and now we had to take a look at our house.

We loved the farm and the idea of what it would become, but truthfully, when we purchased it, the house was a disaster. It had hideous wallpaper, a slope in the floor (you could put a bottle down on the floor on one side of the room and it would beat you to the other side), and the staircase was no more than two feet wide. It was basically a ladder. And there was old teal-blue carpet that was just...tragic.

When we moved in, we were between seasons—not quite winter yet, but not quite still fall. It would snow, then melt, then rain, then get cold, making the surrounding terrain a sludgy mess. People were in and out during the move, animals were in and out as they explored their new digs, and all of this activity was tracking in mud. Mud + ugly teal carpet = a very bad situation. Granted, this might have been a nice touch from Esther's point of view ("Love the new place, Dads!"), but living in a pigpen was not part of our plan when we bought the farm.

The house had apparently been built in stages, which resulted in a plethora of issues we would soon discover. The layout of the house includes the "older than Christ" main house, which is where the dining room, master bedroom, and bathroom are; the upstairs, which is where we'd end up running the Esther Store that first winter; the kitchen, with stairs to the cellar; and a door to an attached (uninsulated) shed that has become the laundry room.

Additionally, there is a sunroom (where our mattress was) and a living room off the kitchen, each room clearly having been added at different times, like a haphazard (emphasis on "hazard") patchwork quilt, with no central heating system at all. And then, as luck and winter would have it, we had our first snow. Pipes froze. The dishwasher froze. We froze.

To heat the place, the previous owners had used big electric radiators that looked like white suitcases, along with two fireplaces, neither of which were up to code. Even with the radiators cranked, the house was still freezing, bringing back memories of the most brutal winter storms on a full-time basis. This was the only time in my life I hoped to be the "second man in" for the bathroom in the morning, for no reason other than that the toilet seat wouldn't be a rind of ice. (I love many more obvious things about Derek, but warming up the loo for me—intentionally or otherwise—is right up there.)

The house was glacial. It got so bad we considered moving everything to the mobile home and just living there, because it at least had a furnace. Imagine that for a minute: two guys, two dogs, two cats, and a 650-pound pig living in their mobile home on the farm. Classy.

Ultimately, it got so cold that we started to use one of the fireplaces, even though our insurance company had told us not to. Esther quickly realized that when the fire was lit, it was the warmest place in the house, so the floor in front of the fireplace became her favorite place to sleep. Once we realized she'd abandoned her bed for this new location, we moved her blankets and mattress over there.

We were starting to settle in. Then, a pipe burst. Of course it did. Why should we have a single moment of peace, albeit freezing peace? The pipe was at the exterior wall of the basement, and to fix it would require someone to brave the crawl space, which no one wanted to do. It was a shallow, messy, terrifying, claustrophobia-inducing area—I was half-convinced bodies were buried under there. "It's like a scene out of a horror movie," I told Derek. "Dirt floor, wild rodents, and spiderwebs that rival the human-catching ones in the barn!"

Derek braved the crawl space. (Let's add that to the many

reasons I love him. Better put it even higher on the list than toasting up the toilet.) But this wasn't a one-time event. The pipes burst again and again. So while Esther was still out of sorts from the move, now we were also feeling out of sorts. (The cats and dogs were fine. The cats were skittish at first but got used to the new place, and the dogs were already thriving.) So each time a pipe burst, we gritted our teeth and made another temporary fix—once we'd decided whose turn it was to confront the Crawl Space of Certain Death. We started using heat-trace tape on the pipes to faux-insulate them, but we finally wound up running two space heaters in the crawl space for the rest of the winter.

By the way, if you're thinking, *Steve, don't you know real estate?! Don't you know houses? Didn't you see this coming?* Well…yes and no. Sure, a first glance at the place told me we had a fixer-upper on our hands. And of course I figured there'd be a surprise or two—that's common in any older structure, much less a place like this. But no, I didn't realize it would be anything like this.

Blame our desperate need to get out of the old house, my excitement about finding a place where we could care for animals, and everything related to those issues. Things happened fast. I was a bit blinded by my passion for our mission. You can see how that can happen. I wish I'd been more prepared for the challenges we'd face, but hey: sometimes you just have to forge ahead and hope for the best.

While all this logistical stuff was happening, and while we were trying to ensure we didn't freeze to death, we were also trying to make sense of our crazy new life: a farm, a hay elevator, and a tractor. You know, agricultural stuff. Here's the problem: We didn't know agricultural stuff. Not in the slightest. We had no clue how to use this equipment, but we suddenly had to learn—and fast. I'd never even been close to a tractor, let alone driven one. So we had a John Deere representative come out to help us get the tractor moving. I asked the rep to give me a lesson, which was not part of his job description, but he was kind enough to give me the most basic of basic visual lessons. He pointed to different things and gave various instructions, none of which I was retaining, but I tried to follow along as best I could.

"You put this shifter here and this shifter here," he explained. "This moves you forward and this moves you back." He showed me how to start the tractor and shut it off. And then he left me to it. He didn't even wait for me to try it—he was just gone. I can't really complain; he'd gone above and beyond the call of duty. But I still felt as if I were on a commercial jet where the pilots had just gotten deathly ill, and suddenly I was being asked to land the thing. Better start your prayers now, passengers.

The tractor has eighteen forward gears and six backward gears. Pretty wild, huh? So you have to pick your speed and your gear. I, of course, put it in the fastest gear and full-out drove from one end of the farm to the other, not realizing I was tearing up the lawn. I was bouncing like crazy (these things don't have good suspension), and I drove around like an absolute fool.

It had snowed a few inches the night before. Not enough that I would ever dream of getting a shovel and manually clearing our driveway had we still been in Georgetown, but on this particular day, I had a new toy at my disposal. And it just happened to have a blade on the back that looked perfect for removing snow. I decided to flex my farmer muscles and show Derek that I could clear a nine-hundred-foot driveway of a dusting of snow in under 3.5 minutes.

Little did I know that the blade thingy has variable height settings, and the one I selected was not the one I should have chosen. In my excitement, I neglected to notice that most of what I was clearing off the driveway was gravel. I had removed almost the entire top layer, exposing the tops of big rocks, and had amassed a really nice eight-inch mound of gravel on the side of the driveway. Derek was working in the barn, so he was unaware of what I was doing, and at first I was also completely unaware that I was drastically reducing the driveway grade. Once I realized it, I knew that when Derek saw what I'd done, he wouldn't be impressed.

I tried to fix it by pulling the gravel back where it had been, but the wheels of our tractor were wider than the blade, so I couldn't get all the gravel without driving in the ditch. I admitted defeat and prepared for the "What the hell were you doing?" speech that I knew was on its way.

To this day we have a lovely little gravel berm the whole length of our driveway, as a reminder that I basically have no idea what the hell I'm doing out here. These are things that can be learned only through experience, which we did not have. We were clearly about to experience a lifetime's worth of firsts.

CHAPTER TWO

L ife on the farm is a bit of a contradiction. There's so much to do at all times with the animals, yet it's a slower life in general. We were used to having friends come over every night for a glass of wine and to hang out. Now it's a huge effort to see our friends, and we don't see them nearly as much as we used to or have much of a social life in general. For the previous couple of years life had been so exciting, the way everything was changing—one bombshell after the next—and a big part of that fun was having people to share it with. It was cool to open that bottle of wine, brace our friends for the newest thrill, and say, "You're not going to believe who called today," or "Guess what just happened?" Suddenly we had nobody there to tell, and we felt the emptiness deeply. I get very emotional about stuff like that. I thrive on people, especially people I like. And while I like Derek, he already knew everything we'd been through! He was there when it happened.

Another big change was adjusting to the loss of convenience

in our new life. When we lived in Georgetown, if we needed anything, Derek would walk the dogs to the grocery store and be home in ten minutes. At the farm, if we needed something from the grocery store, walking wasn't an option. We needed to drive, and it would take at least an hour to get there and back. You don't realize what a difference city living makes until you're no longer there. We can't even have pizza delivered here. If that isn't one of the saddest things you've read today, you don't have enough appreciation for pizza. We're used to not having delivery now, but at first it really sucked.

Also, it felt like my work life had changed overnight. Because we had come to the farm, I (by choice) didn't have any real estate listings. I didn't have any buyers, and for the first time I wasn't looking for them. I'd wake up in the morning and not have clients to answer to, but I'd have a pig to take care of and a fence to build.

The only shame in that fact was that I'd recently made new signs for my business. Formerly, my open house signs portrayed me wearing a kilt (I was "the kilted Realtor"). My new signs were big cutouts of Esther and me, and because I got so busy at the farm, they never got used. I had visions of people just loving my new signs as they'd done in the past. People used to steal my signs all the time, which to me seemed like payback, because I was a very naughty kid and totally would have stolen them if I'd seen them then. When I was a kid, we "borrowed" a life-sized cutout of Britney

Spears from a local convenience store. We'd draw tattoos on Britney and do other potentially inappropriate things… as teenage boys will do to life-sized Britney Spears cutouts. I'd imagine what the kids were doing with my cutout signs and laugh. (I know I don't look like Britney—she has much better hair!)

Both Derek and I were experiencing drastic career changes. Derek was no longer doing magic; his work life went from pulling a rabbit out of a hat on a stage in a city to long days on the farm. For Derek, the biggest change was learning to be so hands-on with animals he'd never previously had to deal with. It was a bit intimidating for him. I was always the "pusher" for these things. The crazy ideas were always my ideas, and I'd dive in with both feet, without a second thought. But Derek came from a grounded, conservative family, and he was overwhelmed. His only previous experience with large animals was hunting them (I know, it's awful, and he'd never consider doing that now), so this was a complete 180.

As time went on and we started getting more helpers and volunteers, we were surrounded by people—that's also not really Derek's thing, so he had to adjust to that too. That's another way in which we're opposites. Derek loves to take a trip that's "just us," while I'm happy to travel in a group of ten. In one sense, coming to the farm took that away from me, because while we have people here all the time, it's not the same as having your friends around. Our staff and volunteers are great, but they're not people I've known for-ever, so it's a different kind of thing.

One of our first volunteers, Ruth, came to the farm about a month or two after we moved in. She had been a very vocal supporter while we lived in Georgetown, and we had conversed with her a few times on Facebook but never actu-ally met until she asked if she could deliver a propane-fueled shower for Esther. Ruth had seen videos of Esther rolling in the mud on our driveway and knew the house was all carpet thanks to our posts about how "pretty" the house was.

She lived about forty-five minutes from us, so it was easy to arrange a time for her to drop by with the shower. When she arrived, she was just a bundle of sunshine. She was so energetic and enthusiastic; her personality was infectious. We had a visit, and she offered to lend a hand in the morn-ings if we wanted. Until then, it was just Derek and me every day; we hadn't brought in any real volunteers aside from friends and family for those first few weeks. The first public event (Get Dirty Day) was planned for the following spring, giving us the winter to do basic preparations before we offi-cially opened. We'd had no intention of bringing on regular volunteers for a while.

But Ruth was so great, and we were already getting the feeling that there wasn't enough time in the day to keep up with what we wanted to get done. We needed help, so we jumped at her offer, and within a couple of weeks Ruth started coming early in the morning to help with breakfast and barn chores.

At first, it was absolutely amazing. Ruth was usually at the farm before we had even woken up, because she was a morning person…and we definitely weren't. Not that we slept until noon, but for us, 8 a.m. was bright and early. Most mornings, by the time we got to the barn, she already had breakfast going, and she'd be chopping produce or washing dishes. It was awesome. She became a real fixture at the farm, and it carried on for months. She had a heart of gold, and all she wanted to do was help, but we soon started seeing little glimpses of trouble.

Ruth was a very sensitive person, and she was incredibly passionate about veganism. But she was relatively new to being vegan. As many of us make that transition and start to learn more about veganism, we become more passionate about speaking up. Ruth started taking that aspect to the extreme, putting stickers on meat products at the grocery store, or pouring fake blood on the display case. That was too aggressive for our style. She was known to be a regular volunteer for us, which meant that as far as we were concerned, her actions reflected on us.

One day, she showed up at the farm in tears, saying she had pulled over a truck full of cows on the highway by signaling the driver. When he stopped, she got out and begged him to let her have the cows. I don't know what she thought she was going to do if he said yes—show up at our place with a tractor-trailer full of spent dairy cows? I totally understood that feeling of helplessness she was describing; I had felt the same way when I saw those snouts peeking out at me on the very same highway.

We live in an area where farming is a very common thing. We see trucks almost every day within minutes of our farm. It's heartbreaking, but at the same time I know I can't go pulling trucks over on one of North America's busiest highways, asking drivers to free their cargo. It doesn't work that way. But Ruth had trouble seeing that sometimes, and no matter how hard we tried to remind her to ask herself, *What would Esther do?* she just couldn't get it under control.

Her behavior aside, Ruth was very dedicated, and Derek and I knew her intentions were nothing but good. So we remained hopeful that we could work through her control issues, rein in her passion, and put her bundles of energy to good work.

Two weeks after the move, we got our first "tall" animals, B.J. and Escalade. They were, respectively, a donkey and a horse who were best friends and needed a new home where they could remain together.

Here's how we got these two: a husband and a wife named Kim and Christine would regularly go out for long drives in the country, and one day they happened upon a horse and a donkey. This sounds like a fairy tale, but it isn't. (You might say the happy ending of it is, but only for B.J. and Escalade.)

In fact, Christine was suffering from a terminal illness, and the long drives the couple took through the country were little mental-health breaks. On one of these drives, they saw the horse and the donkey on a farm, so they stopped to say hello. On a subsequent drive, the couple brought along apples and carrots. This was the routine for a bit. Over time, they really got to know the horse and the donkey, and they started getting to know the owner better too. The farm wasn't the nicest, and the owner was a little rough around the edges and seemed to have a bit of a drinking problem. When Christine and Kim dug a little deeper, talking with some of the farm owner's neighbors, they learned there was some abuse going on. The owner and his friends would get drunk and yell at B.J. and Escalade. They'd drunkenly try to ride them and would generally torment them.

Christine and Kim had known something was wrong. B.J. and Escalade didn't look great: They were quite matted; it was clear they hadn't been brushed in a while. B.J. was calm and very good-natured; he would let you pet and hug him without putting up much of a fuss. But Escalade was clearly damaged. He didn't want any kind of touching. He'd take his carrots from a safe distance and thank you very much, that's it. But the two animals would lie down together, and they were clearly best friends. It was sweet but sad, and Kim and Christine felt helpless.

Luckily, the owner had grown tired of caring for the horse and the donkey entirely, so the next time the couple stopped by, he confided in them that he was putting the animals up for auction. The couple did not like the sound of that, nor the idea of the two being separated. Lots of people want donkeys, but horses are a dime a dozen. It was clear the animals and their bond would not have been protected in an auction situation.

So Kim and Christine asked a friend who had a farm if she would take them, provided the couple came to the farm every week and did whatever was necessary to take care of B.J. and Escalade. Kim obviously planned to do most of the work because of Christine's illness. Their friends agreed, and the original owner was just happy to get rid of the animals, so the couple arranged for a transport from his farm to the new one.

During the transport, while helping Escalade onto the trailer, Kim lost his balance, tripped, and injured his leg. It didn't seem like a huge deal at the time—but when he eventually went to see a doctor, he learned he had bone cancer. It was a terminal diagnosis.

Of course, this was devastating news. Both Christine and Kim were facing the reality that their lives would end in the near future. Obviously, nothing else compared in importance to such an upsetting situation, but the issue of B.J. and Escalade did matter to them, and now they were scrambling to find someone else to help take care of the animals.

Their story was unbelievably inspirational to us. We'd been inspired by all of Esther's fans, of course, and I don't want to suggest that's been anything less than life-changing. But it was amazing how Christine and Kim continued to care so much for Escalade and B.J., even when they'd been dealt the worst news anyone could possibly hear. It was critically important to them that these animals have the best possible life—even as their own lives were ending. It encompassed everything Derek and I feel about animals—that their lives have worth, that their happiness is important, that we as humans have a responsibility to take care of our four-legged friends and do all we can to give them wonderful lives.

The situation lit a fire in Derek and me. We had to build the fences and clean out the stalls, because we had two more animals to rescue. Christine and Kim were counting on us. So were B.J. and Escalade. There was no way we were going to let any of them down.

The animals arrived from Brampton, which is only about forty-five minutes away, but they were hours late because it was hard to get them onto the trailer. Once they did arrive, it took us more than an hour to get Escalade off the trailer. B.J. was easy: he just waltzed right off and into the barn. But Escalade would freak out if anyone stepped onto the trailer. He didn't even have a halter on at that time, so we just had to hope he'd follow us. He didn't.

Nobody was brave enough to hop onto the trailer, which would mean getting behind Escalade. It was up to Derek and me to lure him out. I was using carrots to tempt him to come closer, but that didn't get him out. Then we had a realization:

once we finally gave him space and left him alone, he would want to get out and be close to B.J. He could see and hear B.J. in the barn, and ultimately that was enough to lure Escalade to join him. When he finally stepped out of the trailer, he went straight to the barn and into one of the two stalls we had cleaned out for the pair. He was right next to B.J., and they sniffed each other over the wall. (We didn't want them in the same stall, at least at first, in case they freaked out.)

I just wanted to pet them and cuddle with them. I went into Escalade's stall with some food, and he went nuts. He did not want me anywhere near him. We could touch B.J. a little bit, but Escalade wasn't having it. He was calmer when we stepped back and left him in the company of his buddy; they spent that whole night facing each other in their respective stalls. It was obvious they had to be together. We'd been told we couldn't separate them, but it hadn't made sense to me until I saw them together. Even if it was just a wall between them where they could reach each other's noses, it was still too far apart. These two are soul mates. Even now, if we take B.J. out to trim his hooves, Escalade will run around and scream the whole time until we bring B.J. back.

We put them together in the same stall after a few days, which to them I'm sure was an eternity, and eventually moved them to the "old barn." It's attached to the big barn, but it doesn't have any stalls, so it's a much bigger space. It also has a door to its own little fenced area outside, so they can come and go as they want.

New animals always require attention, and with their distinct personalities there is always a learning curve. We had never been around such large animals, so it was very exciting for me. But Escalade was a wild horse, not a nice, friendly horse as we'd expected. He would spin in circles if you entered his stall and tried to touch him during those first few weeks. We had a farrier come to check his hooves, and he literally behaved like a wild horse such as you see in old westerns, jumping and neighing. I'd never seen anything like it, and he quickly showed us how serious it was to be working with such large animals. It was a huge wake-up call that we were quite possibly in over our heads.

But never ones to give up, we spent hours just sitting in the barn with the donkey and the horse, trying to get them to trust us. B.J. came around fairly quickly and would even let us hug him, but Escalade was quite challenging. It took weeks just to be able to touch him, and it was months before I was finally able to give him a hug. It was a very quick one, but it was still a hug, and I was elated.

As excited as I was the next morning, sipping on my first coffee of the day and reminiscing about my great accomplishment—the Escalade hug—I started to get a strange feeling that something wasn't right. Namely, I hadn't seen my other very large hug partner in quite a while. I'd let Esther out to pee awhile earlier, and after I snapped out of my dreamy Escalade haze, I realized I had no idea where Esther was. I walked outside in my housecoat and flannel pants to take a gander around the property and found a neighbor at the gate honking his horn.

"There's a pig on the road!" he exclaimed, with all the shock and horror you'd expect from a person who'd just driven past a 650-pound pig. In no part of my brain had I considered that she'd escaped our property, and although I was grateful for the information, it was the last thing I wanted to hear. I ran back to the house and yelled to Derek, then immediately took off running, even though I was still in my housecoat and pajamas. I was in pure panic mode.

Derek took the driveway while I went into the woods, so we could cover both paths. I ran clear through the woods and made it to the road without seeing any sign of Esther. I had no idea where she was, and I started to get extremely worried.

You see, we hear guns being fired in this area—people hunt turkeys, coyotes, and God knows what else. I could only imagine some hunter seeing Esther cruise by his back door. I didn't think for a minute he'd hesitate to make a meal of her. Is that a fair assumption? Does it matter? When your little girl is in danger, you don't spend time worrying about that sort of thing. You just want to be sure she's home and safe.

Adrenaline now in full gear, I started running down the road, and that's when I noticed a hint of pink up by our neighbor's driveway, on the opposite side of the road from us. I ran up the hill, finally seeing clearly that yes, it was indeed our Esther. As I reached her, Derek drove right by, not even seeing us. I flagged him down on his second pass; he pulled over, and we devised a plan to lead her back home.

Esther had gone right up to the front door of the neighbor's house and had been digging little holes as she went, doing her thing, rooting, just loving life. Derek was furious, and probably a bit embarrassed (but also scared). This was the first time she had been out, on the road, in a new area full of farmers who would immediately see her as livestock, not a family pet. We hadn't been in the area long enough for the neighbors to know why we were there or that this pig with a gleaming smile was an integral part of our family.

Derek ran back to the house and got plywood, which we used on either side of Esther to guide her back. This is actually a thing. They call these plywood guides pig boards. People use them all the time to guide pigs, but we had obviously never used them before. The idea is that the pig feels like it's in a tunnel with a board on either side, and that helps you usher the pig around. But Esther didn't appreciate them. She was whining and grumbling the whole way. She had no idea what this process was about.

Of course, I thought it was a funny scene and started taking pictures. All of my fears had dissipated once I realized she was okay—funny how my emotions can turn on a dime like that. But Derek isn't wired the same way. He was irate. From his point of view, we were new to the neighborhood, and Esther has a cropped tail. In farmland, nobody would know she's a pet, and this was a near-disaster he couldn't let go of just yet. I was just happy to have my baby back and wanted to document the adventure.

We finally got Esther back on our property, and she had pretty much accepted that we were in charge at this point, so the protesting had settled to the occasional grumble as she headed up the driveway. Derek was still annoyed at both of us, but he was relieved to have her back home. Once we got through the front gate, Esther went straight to the house. She knew we were not happy, but she was pooped, as she had been walking more than she'd ever anticipated.

We got back to the house and gave her a drink, and she settled quickly into her bed. Derek went up to the office, and I lay down next to Esther to see if we could make up. She was fine, and she welcomed me beside her, which was comforting. (I just hate when we argue.) I nestled in close to her and spoke to her as if she understood every word I was saying, telling her that leaving the property was bad, and that she shouldn't do things like that because she could get hurt. I stayed with her for about a half hour and worked on my laptop. But the peace and quiet was short-lived, because we needed to get back outside. As we'd just learned the hard way, we had fences that needed to be repaired immediately.

CHAPTER THREE

n February, Derek's parents arrived for their first real visit since the welcome party on the day we arrived at the farm. I was excited because I knew Brad and Janice were thrilled about the farm—at least I thought they were, especially since they had contributed to our fund-raiser. We showed them the barn and the fences and all the work we'd done so far. Then we came back into the dining room and settled in. Esther was on her bed in the sunroom, Derek went back to the barn to get something, and I had to get something from the trailer outside, so we left Derek's parents to themselves for the moment.

I wasn't gone even ten minutes, but when I came back inside, no one was there. Derek was still outside in the barn, and Esther was in the dining room at the bottom of the stairs. I assumed Brad and Janice had gone out to the barn to be with Derek, so I carried on into the kitchen, without thinking much of it.

Derek came back in a minute later and asked where his

parents were, so I realized they hadn't been with him and that the fact that Esther was standing at the bottom of the stairs was a clue to their whereabouts. Immediately I knew something was wrong, and the look on my face alerted Derek to the same thing.

"Mom? Dad?" he called out.

Brad was upstairs in the makeshift "Esther offices," and he called back as if nothing were going on, said he was "just taking a look around." Janice had barricaded herself in the bathroom on the main floor, behind the door at which Esther was currently sniffing—Esther, of course, smelled their fear. What I didn't know was that Esther had gotten up when I was outside, and she'd started to challenge Derek's parents. When Esther challenges someone she gets pushy. Sometimes she'll physically push you with her head, but usually it's a more subtle intimidation—e.g.: blocking a doorway so you can't get by. This was what she was doing with Janice—blocking the door, grunting, and getting into her personal space. Esther has no respect for personal space when she's challenging. They already were not big fans of our girl, and the challenge led them to plot their own separate escapes, which left them on different floors.

"You can come out, Mom," Derek said. "Don't worry, we fed her already today."

Derek loves to push his mother's buttons. He eggs her on more than anybody. I am so gentle with Janice, but Derek will poke her and prod her until he gets a reaction, which he then finds funny. Derek says he just "asks her questions," but we both know he irritates her on purpose. It's not just about Esther; he does it with everything. All families have their little ways of goofing on one another, but this was not the time to be poking the bear.

We put Esther outside, and once we convinced Derek's parents of that (and that I would take her to the barn), Brad came all the way downstairs, Janice came out of the bathroom, and they both sat uncomfortably at the dining table. Janice's eyes were red, and you could tell she'd been crying. You can also tell when Janice is mad. It's her Scandinavian roots. (She recently did a DNA test and found out she's Scandinavian but insists it's bullshit and that she's from Ireland.)

Brad and Janice were both pretending nothing was wrong, but Derek wouldn't let it go. He kept asking what the problem was, and that's when the waterworks started again.

"What's going on?" Derek asked. "I can see you're upset."

Finally, Janice snapped. "It's the pig! Esther was trying to kill me!"

"Come on!" Derek said. "Of course she wouldn't hurt you."

"She was just sniffing to see who was in the bathroom," I interjected, trying to calm her down. "She's not used to you guys being around; she's just trying to get to know you."

I don't think Janice truly believed Esther would kill her and eat her, but family time with Derek had decreased since the move to the farm, and she was missing her son and perhaps feeling abandoned—and worse, replaced by a pig.

So the Catholic guilt trip came out.

"You care more about the pig being happy than me being happy!" Janice cried. "You love that pig more than your own mother!"

It pretty much became a full-blown yelling match from there. This fight was worse than the one we'd had in George-town at Christmas. (For those who don't know about our previous Christmas, it was a disaster of epic proportions. Brad and Janice brought a deep fryer and insisted on cook-ing a turkey in our vegan home. Fast-forward to now, with Cornelius, our rescue turkey, practically taking up residence in our home, and you can understand why this wouldn't go over well. But somehow this visit started out even worse. At one point, Janice even asked Brad to take her home, but they ended up not leaving. We managed to talk them down—that's when I got more vocal. I usually try to agree and appease when it comes to Brad and Janice, and I usu-ally get quiet when it comes to arguing. I'm always on great terms with them. I rarely get a hug from Brad, but we're never in a bad place.) While I try to keep my mouth shut when it comes to arguments, in this particular case, even I got involved once Janice was repeating her new go-to: "You love a pig more than you love us!"

It got heated, but I was trying to calm them down. I had so hoped things would be better on this visit. In fact, things needed to be better on this visit, or I was worried it would forever set the tone for our relationship with Brad and Jan-ice moving forward, at least for as long as Esther was in the picture. I know everybody likes to make jokes about their in-laws, and how they wish they didn't have to see them. But my relationship had improved so much with both of them since Derek and I had first gotten together, and I really didn't want to lose that. Derek and I both thought the move to the farm would help bring them even closer, because there was so much to do. Brad loves the outdoors and Janice is great at organizing and sorting and all those things moms do so well, so I thought they'd be here all the time.

But it seems that Derek's parents had believed that our buying the house and the farm—with the help of their donation to the fund-raising campaign—meant Esther would now live in the barn with the other animals, and our life would return back to pre-pig normal. They didn't get that Esther was one of us and that this was her house just as much as ours.

This whole scene was doing little to help mend the already-strained relationship Derek's parents had with Esther. Janice was openly expressing how unhappy she was, and she was still irate about the way she'd been portrayed in the first book. I was mortified about that too. I seem to recall her saying the words, "Don't you ever utter my name in public again." (Oops.)

So dinner was tense, to say the least. Janice refused to eat vegan cheese and wouldn't really try anything she wasn't familiar with. It was unpleasant for everyone.

The mobile home on our property is a full living space

with a kitchen, a living room, two bedrooms, and a full bathroom. The whole trailer, except for one guest bedroom, has now been taken over by the Happily Ever Esther Farm Sanctuary (HEEFS) office and the Esther Store shipping department, but at the time Brad and Janice visited, it was just a big, welcoming, pig-free space. We had turned on the water and power in the trailer in anticipation of their visit, so, fortunately, they could go there after dinner, and once they had retreated to the safer space, Esther could come back into the house.

Since then, Brad and Janice have not set foot in our house—they go straight to the trailer or just stay outside. It's not perfect, but at least it means we can have them over, and offer somewhere they'll both feel comfortable while I continue to work on their relationship with Esther. (One day Janice will call Esther her grandpiggy, I can feel it.) Nevertheless, I was super optimistic about where our relationship was heading.

It was a few months before we saw them again, but that next visit was 100 percent better. Janice still wasn't cuddling with Esther by any means, but the weather was warmer, so we could all be outside, and that seemed to make a huge difference. It was the best visit we'd had in years. And then, I think, a real turning point was when they attended the rehearsal for a TEDx Talk we did. It was the first time they'd actually heard us tell our story from the very beginning, and I think they finally got the message.

Still, when we got invited to their house for Christmas

again, I had visions of the Ice Storm Christmas we had spent together in Georgetown. We'd been lucky to even survive that Christmas, so I remained a bit uneasy as the date for this one approached.

Amazingly, when we arrived we were told we would be enjoying a totally vegan Christmas dinner—no turkeys frying beside the house this year. And the vegan dish was not just for us, but for everyone. It was so great. It was probably the single biggest step Derek's parents had made since any of this started, so it was a major milestone, and Derek and I were ecstatic. Our relationship with Brad and Janice has never been better; it seems they finally get why we feel the way we do.

That's not to say they're banging down the door begging to babysit their grandpig, but it doesn't matter. All that matters is that they support us. Derek may never admit it, but I know it drove him crazy to think his parents didn't support him, and I'd guess most children would feel the same way. But they just didn't understand. I think they were afraid we were making a crazy decision by moving to the farm and giving up our jobs so quickly. Things were moving very fast for us, and normally their family would never take a risk like that. It took time to help them see where we were coming from, and for them to realize that we meant business.

Around this time, Esther started to explore the forest. She wanted to check out everything. She also started having a bit of an attitude. Having access to the woods was totally new to her. She had never been able to explore so far from the house before, nor in such interesting surroundings. She didn't want to leave a single stick unturned. We had a pretty good setup by now as far as a perimeter fence was concerned, with only a few gaps still to be filled. But Esther soon realized she could bust right through the fence, so we were constantly trying to stay in front of her and control where she went.

When she did get through the forest fence (always her favorite place to go), we had to place stakes in the ground in front of her, forcing her to turn around. The forest is large, and she wanted to keep going and see it all. She knew we wanted her to go home, but she didn't want to go, and she'd make it clear we were cutting into her "me" time. She'd stand her ground and shout.

It wasn't that we didn't want her to have fun, but it wasn't safe. She could get to the road from there. Also, these areas hadn't been checked for hazards such as garbage and broken glass, so it was really stressful when Esther went into the forest. Not to mention that we almost always had other work to do, and taking a two-hour break to explore the forest, although fun, wasn't what we had in mind for the day.

Whenever it came time to make Esther go home, things would get ugly. She would scream, bite at us, and bite at whatever stick we could find in our attempts to block her path. The first time it happened it was a bit of a shock for us because she'd never done that before. But we knew she was upset, and we tried to roll with it. It became a literal wrestling match, and she always had the upper hoof. Boy, did she become a little gremlin. Or a not-so-little gremlin. More like an angry Smart car coming at you at 40 mph. (Can a Smart car even go that fast?) We'd be guiding her back to the house, and she'd stop and veer off every now and then and turn her head to yell at us.

After one of these forest fights Esther would hold a grudge, sometimes for days. She would be snappy and wouldn't let us cuddle with her, which for me was the worst punishment imaginable. It was heartbreaking, and a total departure from the Esther we knew. I was terrified that this was the end of her happy, playful personality.

We were also worried about what it meant for people visiting the farm. The whole reason we opened the sanctuary was so people could get to know not only Esther, but all farm animals. We knew that hundreds of people were lining up to visit when we opened the sanctuary to the public, and the Esther everybody knew online was not the Esther we were seeing at home. Esther was the very reason people were coming to visit. What if she turned out to be a grumpy, pushy pig? That would do nothing to help us change people's opinion of pigs. It was the opposite of the impression we were trying to give people, and it was the opposite of the Esther we knew.

We were still having moving pains, getting used to being so far away from everyone and everything we'd known. I already felt very guarded, afraid to let certain aspects of our personal lives out into the open. All kinds of people I really didn't know were friending us on Facebook, so even my personal page had become more of an Esther fan page than anything else. Now it was winter, when people often hibernate, but I wasn't ready for friends to visit anyway. We'd moved to a house that really wasn't all that hospitable for guests (at least for the first six months), and I was embarrassed about the house at first, mainly because it was so uncomfortably cold in the winter. It didn't look too bad, other than not being our style (the wallpaper!), but it wasn't a suitable house yet, and it definitely wasn't a cozy place to relax with friends in the living room.

We couldn't leave to visit our friends either, because now we had more animals to worry about. We didn't trust the fences, and we were forever anxious that there would be an escape when we weren't home. Plus, with Esther out of sorts, we didn't trust leaving her home alone either. So we felt very isolated.

I personally think it boiled down to three things: First, some of our friends simply resented our "success." Second, some just didn't get our new lifestyle (which was a legit departure from the Derek and the Steve our friends had known before). And third, in fairness to everyone else, we had become so busy and worried about leaving the animals alone that we had to turn down invitation after invitation.

It felt like there was a wall going up: old friends on one side, all these new people coming in on the other. We did have a great new friend in Krista. We met her through another animal charity when we auctioned off a Tea with Esther, which went for $5,000. (And then the couple that lost offered to match it, so the actual total became $10,000.) In all of the planning and executing, Krista, who ran the charity, became a very good friend and ultimately joined our board. So even though we lost some friends, we gained some awesome friends we'd never have met otherwise.

Still, everything we used to know and do was gone—and even as we write this, it still feels that way at times. We also made some mistakes as we went. For instance, I missed my best friend's housewarming party and noticed a week later she had unfriended me on Facebook. That was very painful for me. Even though we didn't speak very often, I'd always known she was there for me, so to think that all of a sudden she wasn't there really hurt. We have, thankfully, reconnected since then, but the falling-out was a big reminder of what's most important. It's easy to take people for granted, and you often don't realize how important they are until it's too late.

And when all else fails and your friends aren't interested in driving an hour to see you, there's always Ricky Gervais, who's always been a tremendous champion of animals and actually made the trek to visit us. It blew our minds. I felt like such a child that day, waiting at the window to see Ricky and his partner, Jane Fallon—a bestselling author and former TV producer—pull up to the farm. Derek graciously went out to greet them because I was too nervous and excited. It was surreal to see them get out of the car and look around. When I finally did get the courage to walk outside, Ricky and Jane greeted me with a hug and a smile. They were so kind and genuine, much more genuine than I'd have expected of people who were so famous.

I was amazed they knew our animals' names, and they seemed legitimately interested in what we were doing. It really struck Derek when Ricky at one point looked around and asked where our cat Delores was. When they came inside and Ricky saw Esther for the first time he did his famous laugh and said, "Oh God!" just like when he's killing himself laughing on TV. It was incredible; his laugh is beyond infectious. And Jane is just the sweetest. She knew who everyone was, asked questions about how everyone was settling in, and made us feel so comfortable. I now chat back and forth with Jane regularly, even if it's just to say hi, hope all is well. (I really love her.)

And they weren't in a rush either. Sometimes we don't know how long people plan to stay, but they took lots of time to walk around and shoot the breeze. We loved showing them around and taking them to meet the other animals. Ricky was very cautious around the larger ones. We were expecting the arrival of some cows the following day, and Ricky asked about the cows—specifically, if we would have to milk them. We explained that since none of our cows had just given birth, no, we wouldn't be milking them.

That's when we explained the dairy industry to Ricky, in what seemed to be an eye-opening moment for him. We told him that dairy cows are inseminated and then kept pregnant so they are able to lactate. Ricky was surprised to hear that making milk wasn't part of a cow's natural everyday life—a common misconception. He said he'd just believed the marketing all these years. His response was in his facial expression more than in words: he seemed genuinely shocked, and you could almost see the wheels turning in his head. The dairy industry has done an amazing job of making people believe the fallacy that it's harmless. As in, if you got a cow pregnant once, she'd spout milk for the rest of her life. Or as Ricky thought, as if cows just naturally gave milk because that's what cows do. Very smart people (and Ricky is one of the smartest) believe this stuff because it's what we've been led to believe since we were children.

Derek and I always try to be very gentle in how we explain the horrific realities of animal food production, and we never force information down anyone's throat. But if someone asks, we'll let loose with everything we know—even the stuff that can be hard to hear. We think a huge part of our success comes from making people want to ask these difficult questions, and once they actually know the truth, it's very hard for them to turn a blind eye to what goes on. Unfortunately, people believe what they've always believed because that's all they've known, and we all have to be understanding of others and their choices. Traditionally, we are taught that the dairy industry is full of happy cows who live wonderful lives in majestic fields instead of enduring repeated forced impregnation and living in cramped quarters.

Sometimes we feel disappointed by our friends or family who don't become vegan. And as a result, it's sometimes hard to maintain those relationships. It takes a lot of work on our part too to make sure friendships don't suffer. Like I really didn't think my relationship with my best friend would change because I went vegan, but it has. You've got to do everything you can to maintain these relationships, even if it's not the easy way out.

But there are people who have gone further in their beliefs than we have, which makes us look like we're behind the times. For example, the other day we met a vegan who was formerly an organ donor. He has since revoked his donor status because he can't guarantee his organs will end up in the body of a vegan, and he doesn't want his liver or kidneys inside someone who is eating meat. Pretty extreme, right? I mean, how far do you go with this stuff?

People overcomplicate veganism; there is no single answer. It's not just about the animals or the environment or your health, because becoming vegan is triggered by something different for everybody. We all just have to do the best we can to do the least amount of harm. I can't say if Ricky gave up dairy, but he cares so much about animals that I can tell you it got the wheels turning, and he left the farm with a lot to think about.

CHAPTER FOUR

I imagine that for every person, there's a farm animal they know about but have never actually met. For me, that was the cow. It's kind of weird too when you think about how much a part of our everyday lives they are. It's sad but true. People eat them, wear them, even sit on them in their cars and living rooms. But I had never actually met a real live cow before, and I knew nothing about them. I loved cows in theory, and I actually had always wanted a pet cow and thought someday I'd have one (two, actually, and a couple of chickens), so the day the cows arrived was one of the highlights of my life. I'd met goats and sheep before but never a cow, and I was just so excited for the arrival of our first three. (I was even getting one more than I'd dreamed of in my imaginary future.)

It's funny to think I had never even seen a cow up close before. Having lived most of my life so far from rural areas, I had been completely sheltered from farm animals. I was in no way prepared for the size of cows, and their rough tongues blew my mind. I didn't expect that at all. They have giant prickly cat tongues. I had no idea! There was so much I didn't know about them. I didn't know how they liked to be petted. I didn't know how long they lived. So getting to meet one was truly incredible. (I get excited about meeting all animals, but I assure you, this was a special day.) Our three expected arrivals were Denver (a large white ox with horns), Pouty Cow (light brown with white cheeks), and Jasmine (dark brown). They arrived in the winter, so it wasn't a simple task to ready the farm for our new residents.

Like everything else on the farm, the pasture had been unused for many, many years, and it needed to be fenced and readied. There was no way we'd be able to do that in such a short time, particularly in the middle of the cold, snowy winter. So we decided to divide the space we'd already prepped for the pigs, which was about six acres and had access to the barn. We knew the cows had never had access to a barn before, and we had been told not to expect the cows to use it. Regardless, we wanted all the animals to be able to use it, especially when it was cold. So we split the pig pasture and built a fence from the front corner of the barn straight back to the property line, which gave them a big pasture to roam in until we could ready the other, larger pasture in the spring.

You always hear about how farmers are hard at work when the sun comes up, if not sooner. If it wasn't obvious already, well, we're not exactly farmers. We ran a fairly late meal schedule. Breakfast wasn't at the crack of dawn; it was usually at a reasonable hour (to us) like 8 or sometimes 9 a.m., but if we didn't get to the barn by the time Captain Dan the Pig considered an appropriate time, like even ten minutes late, Dan would let us know. He'd walk out of the barn, lift the fence, come into our backyard, step onto our back deck, and yell for his breakfast. He'd literally scream. We'd come out and tell him, "Okay, Dan, we'll feed you now," and he'd follow us back to the barn and behave. But the next day, if it was past a time Dan deemed suitable, he'd be right there at the back door, shouting again. It was hilarious but also a huge pain in the ass.

Captain Dan is bigger than Esther, if you can imagine that. He's eight hundred pounds, so to have this giant pig hollering at you is quite something. Esther would sleep through the whole thing, because she was now settled into the house. She had her own routine, and her own snores probably masked the sounds of Dan's shouting. But Dan was our alarm clock until the day the cows arrived.

You should see the back door. Dan would push at the door, bite at it, and take chunks out of it while he waited for us. There was no doorbell, so Dan's grinding and scratching was the doorbell. That, and the screams. And he'd grunt as soon as we opened the door. He had no patience, that one. So building this new fence put an end to our mornings with Captain Dan. We reinforced the fence he broke through and then there was an extra fence, an extra layer. He'd also have to get through three cows to demand his feeding, and that was too much trouble for Dan. Fortunately.

When the cows arrived at the property, the trailer backed up to the pasture so they could walk right off and into their space. Denver was first off, and when we opened the trailer, I marveled. His butt was to the door, so all I saw was a blinding white wall of ox butt. I couldn't believe how massive he was and that his head would be even higher, somewhere in that truck. Even by ox standards, we've now learned, Denver is very large. So I was just not prepared for this giant guy to be the first thing I saw, nor did I know how he was going to maneuver his way out of the trailer cabin. Somehow he turned himself around. He barely even fit in the trailer, but then I saw him turn his head, his eyes looking at me and his giant horns turned toward me. With surprising grace, all things considered, he managed to get himself facing right-side-out.

Once he saw the door was open, he stepped out. His shoulders were six feet high, and he was actually nine feet tall with his head up. Talk about intimidating. You never think about a cow as such a massive creature, its head towering over you. His horns are more than five feet across. One of them is crooked and curves over his head, so both tips point the same direction. It looks kind of funny, but that's also probably what allowed him to get out of the trailer.

After Denver stepped out, Pouty and Jasmine quickly followed behind. They immediately started to explore the pasture and stopped for hay at the pile we had put out for them. That was when I got to pet them for the first time.

I couldn't pet Denver yet because he was still afraid (I was afraid too, because he was the size of a school bus), but I got to pet the other two and knew that Denver would let me in soon enough. It was a couple of days before I got a lick from them—that's when I learned about their giant cat tongues.

As we had been told, they had no interest in using the makeshift space we had prepared for them in the barn, even when we tried to lure them in using apples or a grain bucket. We also quickly learned how Pouty got his name, because he had an almost constant stream of tears running down his face, and they would freeze into carrot-sized icicles on his cheeks. Snow would pile up on the cows' backs, and we just couldn't understand how they weren't cold. They looked like they were freezing, but they only ever set foot in the barn for a minute or two, then went right back outside. They obviously have a much higher tolerance for cold weather than we do.

For the whole winter, they stayed in the pasture attached to the barn, with B.J. and Escalade in the "old barn" on the opposite end of the building, and the pigs in the middle with a space behind the barn for them to explore. But we already knew we needed to move everyone into bigger spaces, so before the snow even melted, we started planning new fence lines and trying to figure out where everyone should go.

The first couple of months were uneventful. By spring, we thought the animals had settled in, and we'd become very comfortable. Derek and I had been working on fencing the new space for the cows for a few weeks, and we thought it was good to go. It was right beside the pasture they were already using, but it was considerably larger, so we were excited to move them in. But soon after their move, they had their great escape. It happened at the top corner of the pasture, where the cows broke down a fence, crossed the perimeter, and went through the neighbor's backyard (which includes a manicured lawn and a pool). The brazen bovines went up the road a mile and a half, into another neighbor's yard and into the neighbor's woods. That's what we learned later, of course. At the time, we had no idea where they were. We just knew they were gone.

On that particular day, a reality show happened to be filming us on the property. We had been approached really early, even before we moved, about doing the reality show with a different company, but they seemed shady when they casually asked, "So, how often do you guys fight?" What was this, *Real Housewives of Esther's Farm*? No thanks. We didn't proceed because it just wasn't the right time. We had too much going on, and we needed to get everything in order before we could even entertain the idea of having cameras in our faces every day.

By the time we moved to the farm, though, we thought we had more opportunity to provide content that wouldn't involve making a relationship show about us arguing over Esther in our tiny house. We had a lot going on, of course, but we thought the show could be a great opportunity not only to introduce people to Esther but to deepen the connections we were already building online. The show might allow us to introduce a whole new demographic to an "Esther-Approved" lifestyle in a really fun and engaging way.

So we entered into a development deal with a production company that happened to be filming another show just up the road from us. Who knew Campbellville, Ontario, could possibly become a hotbed for reality television? It seemed so random. Anyway, we started shooting a sizzle reel that could be shown to networks while pitching the show idea. (That show never aired. Regardless, the crew was there with us at the farm that day when the cows decided to make a break for it.)

We were filming in the house when Derek excused himself and went outside to feed the cows. That's when he noticed they were missing. (When you're delivering food to animals and there's no one there to eat it, it doesn't take Sherlock Holmes to recognize something's wrong.) The only clue we had to work with was their footprints on the muddy ground.

Derek, our volunteer Ruth, and I scattered to find them, following the footprints through the back of the property. When we got to the property line, it became painfully obvious that the cows had left our farm and gotten onto our neighbor's property. They left big footprints and broken branches in their path, so it was relatively easy to track them until we got across the neighbor's yard and onto the road. Then the footprints stopped.

We couldn't find any signs of them across the road, so we assumed they had taken the road itself, but they had traveled far enough that we couldn't see them in either direction. One of the guys in the film crew came by in his van, I jumped in, and we started driving up and down the road looking for any indication of our missing cows. After a while, he spotted a car on the side of the road with a small group of people assembled beside it holding their cell phones. Turns out I'm not the only one who can't miss a good photo opportunity, and three cows on a tennis court certainly makes for a great photo.

The cows had gone almost half a mile up the road before entering another neighbor's yard, crossing through their tennis courts, and making their way into the forest behind his property. I sent a text to Derek to let him know where we were, then jumped out of the van and started to give chase. The trees were starting to leaf out, so I couldn't see very far. I began seeing signs of broken sticks and branches again as I got closer to the cows, but it was very difficult to see through the undergrowth of the woods. The forest was thick with invasive trees and thorny bushes. They cut me as I ran in search of the cows, and then my sweat made the cuts sting. But my adrenaline was so high at the time that I didn't even notice I was getting cut the whole way. I felt like Kevin Costner in that scene near the end of *The Bodyguard* when he runs from a cabin into the forest. I ran like crazy, hoping I was going the right way, leaping over logs, cutting the crap out of my arms and legs on sticks and thorns. Then I'd stop and listen for the sound of branches breaking as the cows walked. When I heard it, I'd turn and run in the direction of the sound.

Finally, I got close enough that I could see the big white recognizable glow of Denver's butt moving through the bushes. The other two are darker colored and thus were more camouflaged. Once I saw them, I began yelling for Derek or anybody who could hear me while at the same time trying to catch up with the cows and turn them around.

Ruth arrived on the scene, looking like she'd been through a battle. Her face was bleeding, and she had blood dripping down her arms. I think it looked especially bad because it was mixed with sweat and dirt. It wasn't until I asked Ruth if she was okay that she said, "Never mind me, look at yourself." I looked at my shins and they looked like road maps due to the blood and scratch marks everywhere, and all of a sudden the stinging set in because I was now paying attention to it. We didn't have anything but a bottle of water and a dirty shirt to wipe up with, so we cleaned up the best we could now that the hardcore bushwhacking was over. That's when we turned our attention to keeping the cows out of the homeowner's tennis courts.

We corralled the escapees and worked to get them closer to the road, but they settled in between the pool and the tennis court of the very nice house they had chosen to visit. (For the record, Campbellville is a very classy area, with a lot of very wealthy residents, many of whom probably wouldn't take kindly to a group of cows popping in for a game of tennis.) The cows left footprints all over the yard and crapped everywhere. (And these were not simple "cow pies" either: the cows were stressed, so it was very messy poop.) Poor Denver was covered in it.

Ruth called for a trailer to help us move the cows back to the farm, which we were grateful for, but at the same time she was kind of taking over the whole scene. She was telling people what to do, directing the film crew, telling them where they could go and where they couldn't go, and suggesting they assist us with the cows. So while she was helpful in calling for the trailer, we weren't crazy about the idea of her trying to take over an area that was not hers to take over, especially when we were already riled up and trying to get the situation under control. We waited an hour for someone to show up with a trailer, but despite all of our efforts, we were unable to herd the cows into it.

And that's when the police showed up.

Yes, our cows' little adventure had now attracted the attention of the local authorities. As if we hadn't had enough to deal with in the moment. The camera crew probably loved it, but while drama and conflict make great television, they're not so much fun for the people actually dealing with the situation.

We learned that having cows loose so close to the Canadian National Railway train tracks had forced the tracks in that area to be shut down. (Hitting a large cow could potentially derail a train—and you'll recall how huge Denver is.) I was mortified. Derek and I profusely apologized to the cops, who were not amused. The officers told us to "just get the cows." I kept bouncing back and forth between the cows and the cops, trying to provide updates and do everything I could to make sure the police officers weren't mad.

I didn't know how serious any of this actually was, and when the police officers told me CN Railway was holding up trains because of us, I assumed that meant we'd be facing ridiculous fines. Surely this had to be a huge problem for them, and we didn't want this to be our first real introduction to the neighborhood. I was picturing newspaper headlines that read "Esther Opens New Sanctuary, Dads Have No Idea What They're Doing!" or "Pair Fined $10,000 for Disrupting Rail Service with Rogue Bovines."

Since at this point I knew the cows were safe, even though we still needed to get them home, I was more concerned about the ramifications of the day's adventure now that I realized the scale of what had happened. Amazingly enough, the police officers left—to deal with another cow situation! Fortunately, those cows weren't ours, and we suddenly felt a million times better knowing we weren't the only dummies chasing cows around Campbellville that day. It turned out this was actually a fairly common occurrence, so all we got was a stern talking-to. That said, it was still an unbelievably intense day, and we have no intention of reliving it anytime soon.

Five hours later, after many failed attempts with the trailer and much deliberation, we started walking the cows back to our property. We had people on either side of us, a car in front, the trailer behind—cameras rolling, quite a procession. I'd calmed down substantially by that point, so I took a selfie with the cows behind me. But Derek wasn't seeing the humor in the situation yet, so I took only one and then put the iPhone away.

Thus chastised, I sank into my own thoughts. I'd felt a bit better after the police officers left, but I was still tense, and we still didn't have the cows home. The more I thought about what had happened, the worse I felt. What if the cops had felt they needed to shoot the cows? (Of course this is where my mind goes.) How would people have any faith in us as a sanctuary if just weeks after we took in these animals, they escaped and got killed? What if this had meant the end of the Happily Ever Esther Farm Sanctuary? We would have had to sell the farm we just got. I realized how quickly things could go from simply wrong to ruined. All because of a crappy fence.

We finally were closing in on home, thank goodness. But that would be too easy, right? It seemed like the bovine bunch had enjoyed their field trip, their temporary taste of freedom, because they suddenly veered onto the neighbor's property again. But that's not what they actually were thinking. Once we put two and two together, we realized that was the path the cows had taken when they escaped; they were going back the way they'd gone before. We kept trying to get them to the driveway, but they had other plans and cut right through the neighbor's front yard, around the side of the house, and behind their pool, toward the forest that borders our properties.

At least the cows knew their actual destination: Denver and Pouty went right back onto our property. But Jasmine must have gotten spooked. She carried on past the opening and started walking along our back fence, toward the train tracks again. I was screaming for somebody to come help, because Derek and the others had continued on behind Denver and Pouty, assuming I was right behind them pushing Jasmine along. By the time Derek and Ruth realized we were on the other side of the back fence, I was alone with an upset cow who still wanted to follow her friends, despite their being on the other side of a wire fence.

Once Derek and the others got Denver and Pouty safe inside the barn, I yelled to them, asking for wire cutters so I could cut the fence to get Jasmine back in. It felt like I waited forever for them to show up with the cutters—I'm sure it was only a few minutes, but I had no way to keep Jasmine from running off, and I was afraid that she'd get back onto the tracks (they were just fifteen feet away), and what if a train came? Would she run? Would she know which way to turn? Luckily, she stayed with me until I had the cutters in hand. I cut the fence, and I trampled down the bushes to get them low enough for Jasmine to step over, clearing a path for her to get back in. Without too much fuss, she finally stepped over them to rejoin Denver and Pouty.

Honestly, if we'd wanted any of them to get out it would have been Jasmine, because she's the calmest of the cows. She also has something called slipper foot, which makes her hooves curl up like a genie's slipper. It's either genetic or possibly from lack of maintenance, but the advantage to us is that it makes her slower. It's cute but probably a pain for her, so we're trying to fix it with vet trimmings, and slowly but surely, her hooves are getting better.

So for the moment, all was well again... except that we were now left with holes that needed to be repaired: the one they escaped from originally and the new one we had just made for Jasmine. It's all a learning curve. We thought we had the fences built properly, but Captain Dan proved us wrong. So we reinforced and built better fences when we moved the cows to the next pasture, thinking we'd really done it right this time... and then the cows proved us wrong once again. But as we go along and discover all the things we don't know, it just helps us learn and get better. I mean, really. You can't expect a kilted Realtor and a magician to know all this stuff right off the bat, can you?

CHAPTER FIVE

We'd been at the farm for about seven months and thought by now Esther's attitude would be back to normal. We were wrong. Our formerly sweet, laid-back pig-daughter still had a terrible attitude. While we've heard this kind of insolent phase often occurs with teenage girls, we did not expect it with our still-young sow.

It was obvious that we had fence issues everywhere, and nobody seemed more focused on bringing them to our attention than Esther. Attempted jailbreaks were a daily occurrence. Even with me or Derek as a personal escort, she made it her sole purpose in life to find and exploit any weaknesses she came across. She would get funny sometimes: She'd just stop at a spot she knew was questionable and look back at us. It was like she was saying, "You know I can get out there anytime I want, right?" She seemed to be taunting us. Sometimes she'd just remind us she knew there was more to see on the other side of the fence, but she wouldn't push it. Other days, nothing could hold her back.

Since the move, Esther's go-to place has always been the woods. There must be something about the forest floor that pigs absolutely love. The ground is soft, and when she would get out there, she'd constantly look for bugs and roots to eat. We'd seen the same behavior in our backyard in Georgetown, but now it was on a much larger scale. At the farm, we finally got to see firsthand how far a pig will travel in a day when it has the space and the ability to do so. Esther would literally walk for miles, going from one end of the farm to the other. Sometimes she and I would be out for just twenty to thirty minutes, doing a quick lap of the space we intended her to explore. But more often than not, a quick walk would turn into a two-hour adventure.

Esther would get so angry when we told her she couldn't explore wherever she wanted. We'd freed her from the suburbs and introduced her to this wide-open environment, full of mystery and adventure, and here we were reining her in, for fear she'd get hit by a train or shot by a hunter or the police or God knew what else might happen. So we were doing what we thought was best, but as she saw it, we were keeping her from following her dreams. We were those awful parents ruining their teenage children's lives by not allowing them to be free and explore the world.

It kind of reminded me of my parents. When I was in high school, they didn't want me going to outdoor parties with my friends. At the time, I couldn't understand what their problem was, why they were so concerned about a bunch of hormonal teenagers getting their hands on alcohol and having parties in the middle of a forested ravine. What could go wrong?

Granted, I don't think Esther was looking to hook up with a bunch of drunk wild boars in the woods. (Although you'd better believe we'd get a few more great book chapters out of it if she did!) And my parents obviously weren't being as unreasonable as I thought they were at the time, although I'll never admit that to their faces.

With Esther, I suddenly found myself thinking and feeling like any parent who feels they have a problem child on their hands. Everything we were doing to protect her came from a place of love. (OMG, I even sound like my mother. It's worse than I thought!) But seriously, we wanted Esther to have fun and love her new home. The property just wasn't ready for her yet, and she didn't understand that. We felt awful about it, but we had no choice but to get firm with her and make sure we always had eyes on her. We would accompany her everywhere she went. She didn't appreciate the chaperoning one little bit; she'd try to evade us every chance she got. And of course, it was no picnic for us wardens either. It's not like we had all this free time and energy to shadow Esther every time she started to wander—which was often.

I've never been particularly drawn to the idea of being a parent. I've always been an animal person. I like pets. Hell, I love pets. That's my idea of family. Tiny humans...not so much. At first, that was a bit of an issue for Derek and me, because he wanted kids, to the point that it was almost a game-changer for us. Funny enough, over time each of us started coming around to the other's position. I became more willing to start an actual family, while he became less so. Here we are fifteen years later, and still no kids. Well, no human kids.

Either way, I never understood the whole super-protective "keep your kid in a bubble" behavior I had seen from some of my friends. A few years before Esther came along, I was in Amsterdam with my best friend, Michelle—the same friend who would later unfriend me on Facebook for missing a housewarming party. One night, we went on a pub crawl, and at one stop I realized I'd lost sight of her. I eventually found her on the patio, leaning against a wall with a drink in her hand, sobbing like a baby. I was immediately concerned and asked her what was wrong: "Did somebody hurt you? Steal your wallet?" (You know I've always had a flair for dramatics, but I'm even more prone to hyperbole if I've had a drink or two.)

She replied: "I miss my daughter."

Not having expected something so minor to be the problem, I immediately started to laugh. "We've only been gone for a week and a half!" I said. "Get ahold of yourself!" I'm typically a sensitive guy, but I wasn't exactly sober, and this clearly wasn't my finest moment. Later on, I felt bad about it. But to be totally honest, I really didn't understand how you could miss somebody so much that you'd be driven to tears after only ten days apart.

Then Esther entered our lives, and on the first trip Derek and I took that lasted more than a couple of days, I found myself crying my eyes out. I stood on a beach in Negril, Jamaica, watching the most incredible sunset, a piña colada in my hand. And there was Derek, laughing at me while I cried about how much I missed my daughter. My 650-pound, four-legged, snouted daughter. I had become that parent I used to think was so ridiculous, and I never saw it coming.

I should probably take the time to apologize to my parents for being so obnoxiously insistent in my teen years that they were ruining my life, or whining about how mean they were for not letting me do every crazy thing I tried to do. And also to Michelle for laughing at her when she cried. Who would have thought that a pig we couldn't keep out of the woods would be the thing that made me realize what an insensitive jerk I had been?

I wish I knew why that parental feeling had come with Esther. I've always had dogs and cats in my life, and I've loved every single one of them very much. But there's something different about Esther. She's not like a dog or a cat. I don't know if it's her eyes, the particular way she looks at you. Or if it's the way she behaves, that sense of mischief and curiosity we see every day. Maybe it's just the knowledge of what her life could have been, and how guilty I feel for supporting the meat industry for so long. I'm not 100 percent sure exactly what it is, but I am sure there is something undeniably humanlike about her, and it completely changed me. It brought out a feeling of needing to protect her, in a way I assume new parents feel about their infant children. And while I realize it's not easy to protect children in today's world, at least most parents have the advantage of being bigger than their kids. I had a child triple my size (and then some) who desperately wanted to forage in the woods, with all the accompanying dangers.

In a sense, it made me all the more relieved that we finally had her out on a farm, despite the many challenges that came along with it. She must have felt awfully constricted in our small house and backyard. Out here, she could finally be herself. And now, I can't even imagine how horrifying it must be for pigs squeezed into tiny cages at a factory farm. I just wish we could save every pig from that fate.

When we first moved to the farm, I'd leave the house not dressed properly to be out for long, especially in the mornings. I was usually still wearing my super-fancy bathrobe and maybe a pair of plaid flannel pants—assuming the weather required pants, that is—and my new go-to shoes since moving to the farm: Crocs.

I know what you might be thinking: *I can't believe the father of a fashion icon like Esther T. W. Pig wears Crocs!* But if you are, you obviously haven't tried them. They're like little ugly clouds for your feet. Heaven. You're not likely to find me hitting the town in such frightful footwear, but when you're spending several hours a day on pig patrol, your top priority is happy feet, not striking poses on the red carpet. I guess that's just another concession I've made in becoming a "parent."

Anyway, my questionable outfits and I would end up on parade in the forest, Esther loving every minute of it, while I was running through all of the possible things that could go wrong. I'd be trying to figure out if she was going to turn around on her own, or if I was going to need to start World War Pig by turning her around myself. What if she made a run for it and managed to get to the road? I was in a bathrobe, for Christ's sake. Can you imagine this scene when driving to work on a Tuesday morning? You happen across a man in the middle of the road, wearing a robe (probably an open robe), fighting with a 650-pound pig. No one needs to see that, particularly not one of my neighbors. I soon adjusted my outfits to include pants and shirts at all times, if for no other reason than to avoid potentially humiliating situations. I still wore my Crocs, though. You'll have to pry my Crocs off my cold, dead (probably from too much walking) feet.

As the weeks went by, I had also learned that problems would always occur when we were trying to direct Esther. She would get angry when we tried to make her change direction. Sometimes she'd freak out and bite, while other times she'd see that we were going to block her and she'd duck and try to go around us. And she always had the advantage because she was low to the ground. She could burrow under sticks that were poking me in the face, making it incredibly hard to keep up with her. And she's not like a dog—she doesn't like being chased any more than she likes being blocked, so that doesn't help the situation.

But what choice did I have? We had seen previously that the minute Esther thinks she has you beat, you're done for. We couldn't let her win the battle of the woods. If we did, we'd never keep her contained. So we didn't let up, and neither did she. We'd pick up a big stick and block her way with it, using trees to brace one end of the stick, holding the other end so she couldn't pass. She'd bite at the stick and try to run, which we hated, because it was usually across rough terrain.

While that was dangerous for us, our biggest fear was that she would injure herself. We knew that pigs, particularly very large ones, are prone to problems with their legs and hips. It becomes an even bigger problem as they get a bit older. They're bred to grow so large, so quickly, that their joints, ligaments, tendons, and so on can't handle the stress of the weight of their bodies. Also, veterinarians typically aren't as savvy about pigs as they are about dogs and cats, because it's not common for somebody to come in with a 650-pound pig and ask the vet to do thousands of dollars' worth of surgery to fix an injured leg.

I remember a vet who came to our farm to see one of the new pigs from Tara's sanctuary. It was shortly after they arrived, and we were still looking for ways to treat Bear and hopefully get him back on his feet. The regular vet was busy, so he sent a colleague. We had no problem with that—until we told the new vet how old Bear was. He looked back at us, a confused look on his face, and asked, "How long do pigs live?" I couldn't believe he'd asked that question. I didn't know how long pigs lived until we met Esther, but I hadn't spent the better part of a decade getting a degree in veterinary medicine. Wasn't the natural life span of a pig something they should've covered in school? How was this not something he knew—or at least could vaguely estimate?

A similar thing occurred more recently, when an intern at an animal hospital was looking at Esther. He said, "Well you know, at two and a half years, she's getting a bit late in life." I was shocked all over again. All these doctors seem to know are commercial statistics. Yes, two and a half years is "late in life" for a commercially farmed sow. But those are teenage years for a pig who's been allowed to live a natural life. How could they possibly not know that? But they don't. So, when a pig gets injured, it's a really scary proposition, because there's a good chance the vet has never had to deal with it before, or has done it so few times that it's still a learning process. I don't want my pig-daughter to be some doctor's experiment!

I was always so scared that Esther would trip on a tree root, or a little hole in the ground hidden beneath the fallen leaves, and that she'd twist or break a leg. (There's that flair for dramatics again.) I'd get myself all worked up in this terrifying scenario, finding myself thinking of ways I could lift Esther from the bottom of a ravine with her broken leg, so we could whisk her off to Ontario Veterinary College for surgery. I would think all this while she would just be walking toward the forest and hadn't even attempted to cross the fence. What can I say? My mind gets ahead of itself sometimes. So whenever I actually did have to struggle with Esther to keep her in bounds, my worries would go into overdrive.

The worst part: After one of these little fights, she would be mad for days. If you think a relative or significant other can hold a grudge, believe me, they have nothing on a pig. After a big fight, she'd snap at Derek or even at one of the guests. Sometimes she wouldn't let me cuddle with her after a fracas, and I loved to cuddle with her. It was the perfect storm of a teenage pig, with an attitude, in new surroundings. That made it both physically and emotionally challenging for all of us, and we felt the stress all the time.

This behavior change made it really hard to get work done, because I was constantly on the move with Esther. For a large lady, she covers a surprising amount of territory. Bottom line: we really needed those fences to be up and working as soon as possible. I'd have deadlines to meet, but instead I'd be out in the forest with no cell signal or a dead battery, desperately trying to persuade Esther not to cross the road or visit the neighbor's house again.

But as exasperating as her behavior was, I always had to remind myself that she wasn't being "bad"; she was just being herself. We either weren't handling the situation properly or weren't moving fast enough to prevent the problem before it happened. That's what made us feel so guilty. This behavior was her nature. She was biologically programmed to explore, and she was just doing her piggy thing. But we had to say no and be the bad guys, because she didn't understand why she couldn't go to certain areas, and we hadn't mastered pig-speak enough to be able to explain it to her just yet. (Note to self: Rosetta Stone for Pig Communication.)

So why weren't the fences up yet? Well, we knew what we needed to do. There just weren't enough hours in the day. It had never crossed our minds that with all the space we had at this new farm, it still wouldn't be enough. Esther's nature to explore was even stronger than we'd thought. She could freely roam around ten acres, but because she was denied the extra ten acres of the forest, she was livid.

This experience really brought home how brutal existence must be for an unlucky breeding sow—which under ordinary circumstances Esther would have been; she was just lucky not to have that agonizing life. Commercial pigs live in gesta-tion crates that are two and a half by six feet. All they can do is sit or lie down on concrete floors or metal slats mounted to the crates. They can't turn around. Many industrialized barns don't even have windows to offer natural sunlight. The poor animals that live in such barns are completely devoid of any form of stimulation, never mind any chance to explore, satisfy their instinct to root, or build nests for their babies.

And if you can imagine, these pigs live confined like

that for two and a half to three years before finally being butchered. Mother pigs keep their babies for four to six weeks before the babies are taken away to a "finishing barn," where they'll stay until they reach market weight around six to eight months of age. Mom will be left without babies for two weeks before being impregnated again to start the whole cycle over. These sweet creatures can literally be driven into madness from lack of activity and just plain depression. Had Esther been a breeding sow, her life would have been over by now, but here at two and a half years of age, her life at the farm was just beginning.

When Esther was asked to turn around and stop a day's exploration, she wasn't just irritated, she was furious. Curbing her impulse to roam was not like dealing with a dog. You yell at the dog, it knows it has misbehaved, and then it's over. Esther's drive to investigate and dig was so strong that it led to major physical altercations. To then think about how commercial farm pigs are treated and what they must feel is heartbreaking, especially when you think of how smart these animals are. You have to consider what's going through their minds as they're trapped in these prisons.

Only a few kinds of animals can recognize themselves in their reflection and understand the function of a mirror—pigs, dolphins, chimpanzees, and humans. Dogs think mirrors are windows. (Then again, dogs think poop is food, so it could be worse.) Pigs are so much smarter than most people realize. Studies at Pennsylvania State University have shown that pigs learn to play video games as fast as chimpanzees and more quickly than three-year-olds (children, not animals). The pigs use their snouts to move the joystick and play the games with more focus and success than chimps do.

We've never tried to replicate any of the experiments we've read about online, but we can easily see how their results apply to Esther. At our old house, we marveled at her ability to open doors that were completely shut. She figured out how to easily operate a lever-style door handle with just her snout. We had never taught her that; she figured it out on her own. She did the same when we moved. A few days after we arrived, she could fling open the sliding patio door to go outside for a pee. We didn't even have sliding doors at our old house, yet she mastered these almost immediately.

We often compare her to the dogs, particularly because of how she plays with her treat ball. The dogs have always had treat balls, and they always did the same thing with them. A dog would roll the ball around for a few minutes, but once the ball would get stuck somewhere, or the dog would get bored, the dog would just abandon it. Or else the dog would bark until we came and got the ball. But Esther would take a treat ball and walk in a straight line from one end of the room to the other until it was empty of treats. There was no comparison in her ability to master toys or solve problems. We had never seen anything like it. It was obvious that pigs are cognitively sophisticated creatures with a much deeper level of thought processing than we ever could have imagined.

It's hard to think of all the unlucky pigs out there when we consider how much we love our girl. And that is still a huge part of why we continue our mission. But with this move and Esther's sudden behavior shift, I was starting to worry that the sweet little girl we knew and loved was gone. Beyond all of the logistical struggles with Esther's explorations and our disagreements, I was extremely upset about her attitude. This wasn't the pig I'd come to know. I worried that Esther was forever changed—or worse, that the rumors about how mean pigs can be actually might be true.

I must admit there was another consideration as well: We had been presenting this image of Esther online that was nothing but sunshine and roses, and that had been perfectly accurate in her early years. But "teenage" Esther was a serious departure from the Esther everyone else knew and loved. Thousands of people had just helped us get to the farm, and we knew many had plans to visit and meet the star attraction. They'd fallen in love with this sweet girl, just as Derek and I had. It would change everything if they came out to meet her and she chased them. Or, heaven forbid, if she became extremely aggressive toward them—which certainly was a possibility, the way things were going. We wanted people to meet the Esther we'd known all this time, and she was making it really hard to arrange that. If her obstinate— her literally pigheaded—behavior continued, we had no idea what we were going to do.

CHAPTER SIX

When you have pigs and cows and a donkey and a horse, you might think to yourself: *What I really need is some goats in my life.*

Granted, you probably don't think that. You probably don't have all those animals, and even if you do, having the phrase "some goats in my life" cross your mind is unlikely. Hey, I get it. We live an atypical life. And then some.

I honestly hadn't been pondering the overall pros and cons of goat ownership. But that didn't stop the impending goat arrival—or the additional pig who was tossed in for good measure.

We got them in a somewhat convoluted way. They were coming from a small family farm in Sudbury, a few hours north of Toronto. I thought the farm was closing due to financial difficulties, that the farm owners were going to lose everything and because of that, they had agreed to give us the goats. From what I understood, the farm previously had been operating as a dairy farm, but the owners had fallen on hard times and were going to slaughter the goats themselves or send them to market. I thought we were saving them.

It wasn't until later that I learned our volunteers had paid for the goats. Had we known this was the plan, we wouldn't have let it happen. We never should have allowed those animals to be purchased, for so many reasons. Animals should never be purchased. When you buy an animal from a farmer, you're just facilitating the purchase of another one. You didn't really rescue an animal, so much as you took one out and let another be purchased in its place. But we were still learning how to run a charity and didn't know all the rules yet.

We had no idea how complicated it was going to be to get our charitable status. We hired a lawyer to prepare our application and spent thousands of dollars, only to get a rejection letter that was literally fourteen pages long. Basically everything we wanted to do was deemed "not charitable" by the Canada Revenue Agency (CRA), the Canadian version of America's Internal Revenue Service.

The CRA even went as far as saying, "You should just register as a zoo; it would be much simpler for you." They just didn't get it. A zoo? Seriously? They told us that rescuing an animal that was eligible for slaughter was against the rules. Slaughtering animals is obviously legal, and the CRA wouldn't let us advocate against that. We couldn't promote veganism, we couldn't run a community garden, we couldn't do almost any of the things we wanted to do.

So we needed to get creative. We were lucky in that we

already had an organization called Esther the Wonder Pig that was completely separate from the charity we were trying to create. We had to ensure an iron wall went up between the two organizations, letting Esther the Wonder Pig do all the things we weren't allowed to do as a charity. We had to ensure that the charity's board of directors was not controlled by Derek and me, so we brought in people with an arm's-length relationship to us—people who shared the same values and objectives but wouldn't be afraid to tell us no if we wanted to do something that could jeopardize our charitable status.

The sanctuary was barely up and running, and we were already losing control of it, just to satisfy the demands from the CRA. But we knew we were being scrutinized and that we would continue to be scrutinized even after we got our status. So we had no choice but to do everything we possibly could to meet the CRA's criteria, while remaining true to our objectives and ourselves. It would end up taking almost two years, but we stuck to our guns, and eventually we became a registered charity as a farm sanctuary.

But that was later. At the time of the goat purchase, we weren't quite there yet. We hadn't learned all the ins and outs of accepting animals, so we were playing it by ear. We were expecting three goats: William, Catherine, and her baby, George. Yes, we named them after royalty because what royal family doesn't want to be likened to a family of goats? We sent a team to the farm to get the goats, but when our volunteers got there, they found a pig by herself in a barn, which seemed odd to them. When they asked the farmers what was up with the pig, they said she was heading to market. (Those are words we rescue people never want to hear.) One of the volunteers mentioned that the pig looked pregnant, and the farmer agreed, but he couldn't confirm that (and didn't seem to care). The farmer definitely wasn't letting that get in the way of sending the pig to market. Our team couldn't stand the thought of leaving her behind, so they convinced the farmer to let her go, as long as we would agree to take her.

The volunteer who called us couldn't tell us much about the situation, just asked if we could take the pig, presuming the farmer would give her up. Derek and I spoke briefly, knowing time was of the essence, and agreed we could handle an extra head, especially when we knew it was either us or the slaughterhouse. When we got the call that the farmer was in fact giving up the pig to us, we thought, *Great*. But then when we found out that she might be pregnant, we started to worry a little bit.

We could handle one pig, but pigs can have litters of upward of fourteen piglets. We weren't prepared to take on something like that, but how could we say no now? We started to ask more questions, but we didn't get much in the way of reassurance or even a solid answer as to whether she was pregnant. Regardless, we knew what we had to do: we would have to just figure it out like we always did. That pig was coming home to us no matter what.

Moving day, and a final wave to our little house in Georgetown.

Shouldn't I wait until the red carpet gets ̶led out? *Photo credit Jo-Anne McArthur.*

Getting moved in. Now we just need to find the screwdrivers so we can assemble our bed.

So, what are we supposed to do with it now?

Met the neighbors. A bit prickly but generally quite pleasant.

Our future chicken coop, assuming the building can be salvaged. The back wall was built using wood from old railwa boxcars. There's no way we'd let it go without a fight.

That carpet cleaner works harder than anybody I know.

The fridge is my favorite thing in our new house.

♪Hangin' tough ♪. Bobbie, the New Kid on the Block, at Happily Ever Esther.

Is that pasta I smell?

B.J. and Escalade, best friends forever.

I still don't understand why we didn't move to the Bahamas.

Sir Denver,
the Gentle
Giant.

I'm afraid all of the
beds are spoken
for this evening,
but you might find
a sofa in the living
room.

The United
Colors of
HEEFS.

I'm so bored, let's eat something.

"Kindness is like snow—it beautifies everything it covers." —Kahlil Gibran.

The Royals: William, Catherine, and Baby George. (Diablo and Debbie are in the background.)

Stopped at our favorite drive-through for a couple of chai lattes and one of those fancy breakfast bars with all the seeds.

Take off that ridiculous poncho, or I'll take it off for you.

I'm running because I don't want the paparazzi to see me walking with somebody wearing Crocs and socks.

Fashion is what you buy; style is what you do with it.

Be the reason someone smiles.

Changing the world one heart at a time.

When the new pig arrived and we got a look at her, we weren't convinced she was pregnant. She couldn't have been more than two years old, we thought, which would make her just barely able to get pregnant. Nevertheless, we scheduled an appointment with the vet for a few days later. But two days later, on April 1, when Derek and I were taking some friends into the barn to show off the animals, Derek immediately yelled, "She's having babies!" Of course, knowing full well it was April Fools' Day, I told Derek to fuck off. I didn't believe for a second that he was telling the truth. But then Derek held up a slimy little piglet with the most hilarious expression on his face.

We all started to panic. I immediately grabbed my phone and called the vet to tell him the piglets were coming. He said, "Okay, let me know if you have any problems." My response: "This pig is having babies. We've never delivered babies. That is a problem!" The vet laughed and tried to calm me down, explaining that there was nothing we could do except comfort the mother and help catch the babies as they arrived.

It was a pretty incredible experience. Eight pigs were born, one of which was stillborn due to a very rare physical disorder. We soon lost two more just because they weren't strong enough; no matter what we tried, we just couldn't get them to pull through. But both of the piglets we lost passed away comfortably in our arms, and they knew nothing but love. They were buried together in one plot on the farm, in a small marked grave in the forest where they would've played with their mom and siblings. The five surviving piglets have been thriving ever since, and each weigh about three hundred pounds now! And we named the mom "April," considering the auspicious, if not ridiculous, day she had her litter.

We were concerned about having piglets on the farm, having heard so many excuses for why commercial farms use gestation crates. They say the mother pigs will step on or roll over onto their babies, crushing them to death. The piglets were tiny when they first arrived, and once the vet examined them and April, he said she had likely given birth prematurely, potentially as a result of stress from the move. Since we obviously weren't using gestation crates, we were afraid April would crush her babies. So we were incredibly careful, keeping constant watch over them.

For the first few days, we kept the piglets in a large wooden box beside their mom, taking them out every couple of hours to let them feed and walk around. April was always super gentle with her babies... and protective. As soon as we started lifting them out of the box, Mom would come over and lie down. Then she would start making these really funny honks and grunts, which is apparently called "singing" for pigs, although I can't lie—it's not the prettiest of tunes. But the piglets know exactly what that means: dinnertime! The whole time they fed, she would keep the noises going. It was incredible to watch, and the look on April's face was amazing. We weren't sure how many litters, if any, she'd had before and experienced their being taken away. But we knew she was going to be keeping these babies, and that felt wonderful.

Eventually we decided to build a small space in the corner of the stall where the piglets could go but Mom couldn't fit, to give the piglets an area where Mom couldn't accidentally smother them. There also was a heat lamp in there, and the piglets loved it. They love to be cozy, so we knew the heat lamp would attract them. Mom would still be close, but the little corner area was a totally safe place where accidents couldn't happen.

We were under a microscope, scrutinized not only by other sanctuaries that might have been a bit jealous of our success, but also by farmers and industry people who would have loved the opportunity to say, "Look how badly those idiots screwed up." We were trying to dispel myths about pigs, and we wouldn't be doing anyone—particularly the pigs—any favors if we screwed up and cost those piglets their lives because we hadn't done the right thing. It's hard to live under so much surveillance. You know the vast majority of people are cheering you on, but there's always someone in the shadows who can't wait for you to fail. We weren't going to give them the satisfaction.

Unlike April and her piglets, the goats were already a family when they arrived, so it was really neat to be able to keep them together. Goat and cow dairy farms operate the same way in that the animals produce milk only when they have babies. The babies get taken away; the male goats are raised to be meat goats, and the females are turned into future dairy goats. Very rarely, if ever, would they be kept together. Catherine had just given birth to her baby, George. William was the stud. When they carried George off the trailer he was tiny, about the size of our dog Reuben, and still nursing. Now that Catherine was at our farm, not only would she not be forced to have another baby, but she would get to keep this one. Keeping the mom, dad, and baby together was a rare situation. William, being the stud, probably had many "wives," but when they came to us, Catherine got to be the only wife.

When they first arrived, we decided to put them in the forest pen. It turned out goats are even worse with fencing than pigs and cows—not because they break the fences but because they jump over them. Catherine would climb up a big rock five feet away from the fence and leap over the fence to get to us. We used to joke that she was the worst mother in the world, because every single day, we'd be in the barn with the animals, and suddenly Catherine would appear at the back door of the barn. At the time, we thought it was hilarious that Catherine would just abandon William and George and that they were too scared to make the leap.

There were times we'd be done with breakfast and doing errands or whatever, and Catherine would be grazing in the grass and doing her goat thing for up to two hours, while poor George was starving. Catherine seemed to prefer to spend her time with people in the barn, while poor William and George looked on from the fence.

William did not take this betrayal lightly. He would always make a big fuss, alerting us to Catherine's absence really quickly. He was such a tattletale. And when we walked Catherine back to the pen, William would greet us at the gate with his little tail just wagging away. We never knew if he was happy to see Catherine return, or if he was laughing at her because she got brought back to the pen. Probably a bit of both, we thought. This went on for a while, until we moved them into the pasture where the pigs were, an area that didn't have a rock close enough for Catherine to launch herself over the fence.

In this instance of fence debacle, we hadn't failed. We just hadn't thought of animals leaping. A friend of ours made a joke that's apparently an old saying: "If it can't hold water, it can't hold a goat." We hadn't heard that one before, but it's definitely true. Goats are the Houdinis of the farm animal world. So this became our new challenge. We had finally succeeded in building fencing that kept our other animals in, and now we had these escape artists to deal with. But once we got the goats into a pen that didn't have rocks Catherine could climb, things were under control. She'd stay put, so George had his mom there for nursing.

The way George would feed was ridiculous. Goats head-butt things, as I'm sure you know. He'd put his head down and ram Catherine at full speed, right in her crotch—I'm not sure why—but then he'd make his way to her nipples. As silly and painful as it looked for her, that was George's source of food. He fed off her religiously for four months, well past what we'd believed was acceptable. His little horns were growing in, and he was almost half Catherine's size, and by that point she was trying to wean him. George didn't care. He kept coming back and ramming her for more. After a while, she wanted nothing to do with it. (Can you blame her?) She'd kick her leg and run away from him with one leg in the air, and he'd be hanging on to her with a nipple still in his mouth. It was awkward, like those pictures you see where the way-too-old kid is still on the nipple. I'm all for breast-feeding, but when you can walk up and ask your mom to whip out her boob, I think maybe it's time to stop. That's how it was with George and Catherine.

But it's worth noting that we had this dairy baby who wasn't taken away from his mother at a couple of weeks, as dairy babies normally are, so we got to see the whole process. We watched George nurse for as long as he wanted—or as long as Catherine would tolerate it—and then grow to be happy and healthy. To this day, they're inseparable. They sleep together, graze together, play together. It's the sweetest thing.

The situation with William, however, turned out not to be as good. I loved William; he was so sweet, and he and the other goats were the first animals we got from a true commercial setting, so I knew William had had a hard life. I was ecstatic to be able to give this goat a happy, peaceful retirement. William was hilarious, and he was an awesome dad. When Catherine was constantly escaping from their pen, William always stayed behind with baby George and took care of him. He was more like a dog than a goat, always affectionate, loved to be scratched or petted, and would follow you around pretty much everywhere you went.

Then one day we noticed something was wrong. William just wasn't himself. He was usually very social and always came up to say hi when you went into his stall, but now he was keeping to himself, not his usual happy-to-see-you goat self. He also seemed uneasy on his feet, a little bit wobbly.

I called the vet out to take a look, hoping maybe it was just a virus or something. The vet tried treating William with meds, but we soon learned William had a disease called caprine arthritis encephalitis virus (CAEV), which is actually from the same family of viruses as HIV. The vet said we would have to put him down.

I hadn't known about this goat disease. These were our first goats, and we'd done only a basic vet check. We didn't have any other goats yet, so we didn't quarantine them or do any of the procedures we do now when we take in new animals. Not that it would have made a difference.

The way this went down, we didn't really understand what was happening. William was limping a little bit one day, and we just thought, *Well, goats are goats. He's climbing and jumping, he probably just needs stall rest.* But that wasn't the case. This was heartbreaking. I was gutted.

I had expected to have him here much longer. I felt like

William had just arrived, and he didn't get to experience as much of a free life as we'd hoped he would. In my hokey vision of life on a farm, I pictured being best friends with all my animals. I imagined walking around with my goat and my pig and my cows all following me, and William fit that bill. George was a wily little bugger, and Catherine would abandon her family without giving it a second thought, but William was my pal. He was so calm and loving; he just wanted to be touched. The minute you walked into his pen, he'd walk up and stand right at your legs and touch you with his shoulder, and then he'd nuzzle up against you and rub his face on your leg. He didn't want to wrestle or chase or head-butt you. He wanted to be your pet. He would run over when he saw you and always wanted to be cuddled. He was like a dog-goat to me.

He'd been on our farm only about six months, so we hadn't even considered death as part of the process. It just wasn't on my radar—but this was a stark reminder that the more animals we had, the more often we would have to say good-bye to them. You always know that, of course, but you can't really prepare for or figure out how to handle it. Moreover, because these are sanctuary animals, I thought I'd remain a step back from them. I thought I could keep myself at arm's length and believe these were not my pets. (I guess that's hard to do when a pig is an integral part of your immediate family.) We're rescuing these animals, but they're not part of our immediate family. I'd do anything I could to try to detach a tiny bit, because I knew that if I got too attached and lost an animal, that sense of loss would shut me down.

But even with all the mental preparation I thought I'd done, William's death hit me really hard. I realized it was going to be a lot more difficult than I'd thought to keep my chin up and not get too emotionally entangled when these things happened. But it was something I knew I would have to learn to deal with if this was going to be my life from now on.

People ask what's the hardest thing about running a sanctuary. It turns out everything is hard, whether it's losing an animal or dealing with a financial concern—the unknown about where your next dollar is going to come from—or regretfully having to say no to taking in an animal. That last one is something I'm not well equipped to handle. I'd never thought about how much of an emotional drain it would be to say no, but we can't take every animal, and some people, as a result, can be really cruel. They'll say, "If you don't take this animal, it's going to be put down—this death will be on your hands." That's pretty harsh when you're trying to do a good thing and simply can't save every animal in the world.

I was not ready for William to go. Watching him deteriorate over those last few days, hoping he'd get better but knowing he wouldn't—that was one of the most painful things I'd ever experienced. We had to put him down. You never want to think of having to make that call for somebody, to say, "Today's the day." Scheduling a death is not easy, even when you know it's for the better. Knowing you're going to lose someone is different from knowing you're going to lose that someone at 1 p.m. It's tough, but it's part of the deal.

William was cremated and joined the piglets in a plot on the farm. We told him that the Happily Ever Esther Farm Sanctuary would be his home forever, and that held true even after he passed away.

CHAPTER SEVEN

As beautiful as the farm was...it was a mess. Sure, before we'd even taken possession of the property, I'd noticed a few pockets of rubbish in various places. So I knew we had some cleanup ahead of us. But we had completely underestimated the scale of the task at hand. It seemed like everywhere Esther would dig, she'd unearth broken bottles or tiny slivers of rusted-out metal. Not exactly buried treasure, in other words, no matter how exciting these shiny discoveries might have been for her (or terrifying for us).

I guess in the old days, it was acceptable practice to turn your property into your own personal garbage dump. Or maybe lack of access to regular weekly trash pickup back in the early 1900s had something to do with it, especially in a rural area such as this. Regardless, by the time we moved in, most of the glass and metal had been buried under years of dirt and overgrowth. I'm sure most of it never would have been seen again if not for our darling girl with the built-in rototiller on her face.

Esther's always had a knack for getting into things she's not supposed to, so why would broken glass be any different? I mean, love her as we do, and we do very much, at the end of the day she happened to be born a pig. And a pig's gonna be a pig.

On one of our daily walks, I noticed Esther had a bit of a limp. It didn't seem serious per se—it's not completely out of the norm for her to occasionally favor one leg a bit, as we all do—but she obviously wasn't feeling quite like herself. We looked her over and assumed things would improve by morning. But the next day she showed no noticeable improvement, so we called our vet. In typical fashion, I started to assume the worst, and I've learned that it's usually best if I just call in somebody who can talk me down from the edge of hysteria. (At least temporarily, because with apologies to Aerosmith, most of the time I'm livin' on the edge.)

Dr. Kirkham arrived around 8 p.m., when Esther was already settled happily on her bed in front of the fireplace. We had gone for our walk, she'd eaten dinner, and everything seemed pretty much normal, aside from the limp. The doctor examined the leg in question. He checked out her foot, knee, and shoulder, and again everything seemed okay. She clearly had some discomfort, but it looked like a muscle issue, as we had initially suspected, so our minds were put at ease for the moment. We decided to just give Esther some quiet time and not encourage her to tag along for walks as we usually did. (Of course, that's easier said than done when the young lady wants to join us.) But the doctor's recommendation was bed rest, so we had to keep her as inactive as possible for a few days while whatever was bothering her sorted itself out.

Keeping Esther inactive was no small task, but it was certainly better than the other scenarios playing out in my mind. It all seemed like a pretty straightforward situation when Derek and I went to bed that night. But that changed when I woke up the next day and went into the living room. Nothing I could say would get Esther up and into the kitchen for her morning juice.

(Yes, she still drinks her juice every morning. It's a very diluted iced-tea mix, but it can't be diluted too much, or it won't pass inspection, and thus it ends up angrily spilled across the kitchen floor. It's one of her diva demands, along with memory foam mattresses and no noise after 10 p.m. And yes, she's spoiled. Americans have their Kardashians. We have Esther.)

When Esther wouldn't get going, I started getting worried, of course. And just because that's often my natural state doesn't mean my concerns aren't valid on occasion. But I tried not to think about the limp she'd had. Esther is known to be more of an afternoon pig than a morning pig on the best of days, so her behavior this time wasn't entirely out of character. Imagine trying to rouse a fussy teenager who just wants to sleep in on a Saturday morning, and you'll get the picture.

I got behind her and started gently but firmly poking either side of her butt with my index fingers, saying, "Come on, Boo Boo, piggy breakfast time." She hates being prodded out of bed, so I knew that would get her moving, and it definitely did. But when she leaned forward and lifted her back end to stand up, her front end collapsed, and she fell forward onto her face, squealing in pain. She tried to get up again, but she couldn't get her footing, and her legs kept slipping out from under her.

I'd never seen her have this kind of trouble before, and it was terrifying. This was truly unprecedented: something was seriously wrong with my little big girl. My heart was in my throat. I screamed for Derek and tried to help her get up, but she was way too big for me to really do anything but support her a bit. There's no way I could actually lift her enough to help stabilize her feet. I felt like one of those mothers summoning superhuman strength to lift an overturned car off one of my children, but in this case the car was my child. By this point she was flopping on the floor like a captured tuna on the deck of a fishing boat. Every time she tried to put her foot down, she'd pull it up in pain and fall right over again, causing her to panic as much as I did. It felt like the scariest few minutes of my life, although in reality it was only a few seconds, because Derek had heard my scream and the commotion and came flying into the room like the house was on fire.

As soon as he saw Esther and the trouble she was having, Derek was in just as much of a panic as I was. He immediately called our vet's office, and they instantly got the message that it was an emergency, because they had Dr. Kirkham on the phone right away. Derek explained the situation, and Dr. Kirkham told us Esther needed to go to Ontario Veterinary College (OVC, at the University of Guelph) immediately. We weren't about to argue, so we confirmed he should make the necessary calls and get us in as soon as possible.

But there was one complication. (It seems like there's always at least one.) We didn't own a trailer. In other words, at that very moment, we had no way of transporting our 650-pound girl to the hospital, which is eighteen miles from the farm. You might think that's something we should have thought of before this, and believe me, we agree. But like so many other things on our insanely long to-do list, it simply hadn't been done yet. It's a list, after all. You cross things off as you go, as quickly as you reasonably can, and that one was still on there. It hadn't seemed like the biggest concern—until it was suddenly the greatest concern we could imagine.

We had to come up with something fast. I knew it was serious when the vet was as concerned as I was. I called Ray, a real estate friend. I knew he used an enclosed trailer to move furniture in and out of houses for sale when staging his listings to make them look better to prospective buyers. His trailer was available, but he wasn't. He was out of town at the moment. We had to call around to find someone who could go to Georgetown and pick up the trailer, then drive to Campbellville to pick up the three of us, and then drive at warp speed (but a really safe warp speed) to the hospital. In total, it would be about an hour and a half of driving, depending on where the person lived who agreed to do it. Derek and I are really lucky, because we have the most amazing friends in the world. After just a few phone calls, we found someone who dropped everything to help us out.

While we were zipping across town to pick up the trailer, our vet was making arrangements with the hospital. He called while we were still on our way to Georgetown, letting us know that OVC had agreed to take Esther that same morning. But there were three conditions that came along with the agreement: we couldn't take photos, we couldn't bring any guests, and we couldn't spend the night. It seemed our reputation had preceded us, but I knew there was no choice. I agreed to their rules, even though I had no intention of following one of them. No guests? Okay. No photos? Fine. But leaving her alone in a strange place, with strange (to her) people? That was not going to happen. Not in a million years. I think Dr. Kirkham knew I felt that way too, but he had to relay what OVC told him, and he knew I knew I had to agree . . . at least until we got there. Formalities.

We finally got the trailer, made it back to the farm, and got Esther loaded up. Remarkably, given her condition, that wasn't too tricky. We backed up the trailer right to our back deck by the sliding door, and then dropped the ramp directly onto the deck itself. Esther didn't even have to step up to get into the trailer. It was a straight line and as easy as we could possibly make it for her. With a little encouragement, she hopped and hobbled into the trailer without argument. But every step broke my heart a little more, because I could tell that every step she took was torture. We had prepared the trailer as best we could, with plenty of straw and some of her favorite blankets, so she would be as comfortable as possible. As soon as all four of her hooves were in the straw, she lay down with a big sigh. Derek and I followed her in and lay beside her, riding in the trailer with her for the entire trip.

On the way to the hospital, I called our close friend Krista, who has worked in animal rescue. I just wanted to let her know what was going on, but our brief conversation turned into her giving me a twenty-minute speech about how much money the animal-agriculture industry donates to OVC, the testing that goes on, and ultimately where she believed OVC's interests lay. By the end of the call, Krista had me convinced that OVC was basically working for the animal-agriculture industry and that the people there would kill Esther at the earliest opportunity they got. It was the last thing my overactive imagination needed to hear.

I'm sure Krista had not intended to upset me, but she's such an encyclopedia of information, she often answers my questions a little too well. And like most of what goes on in the world of animal agriculture, it's almost better when you don't know the truth. The world seemed like a much kinder place when I lived in my bubble. Every time I learn something new about what our laws have deemed to be an acceptable practice, I realize how cruel we humans really are.

Esther is a threat to the animal-agriculture industry, and we know that because we've started showing up in industry magazines suggesting how "ridiculous" we are. And after that conversation with Krista, I felt like I was handing Esther over to the enemy. My panic level jumped off the charts in a heartbeat. And because I arrived at the hospital fresh off the phone with Krista—and emotional because my baby girl was lying in agony on the floor of a trailer—I admit, I was no peach to deal with.

At the hospital, I questioned everything the doctors said. I even called Susie Coston at Farm Sanctuary and Rich Hoyle from the Pig Preserve to ask for their thoughts on every little detail. I'd tell them what the doctor had said, what medication he wanted to use, or what procedures he was considering. Then I'd go back to the medical team at OVC and say, "Well, Susie says" this, or "Rich says" that. I was basically every doctor's worst nightmare—animal doctor or otherwise.

Keep in mind that this is one of the best veterinary schools in the world, and here I was questioning the physicians' every move. Things really came to a head when they said they wanted to sedate Esther for X-rays. That's when my mind went into overdrive, and I basically lost it. Aside from the typical health concerns that come with pigs, another very serious issue is hyperthermia, which just means dangerous overheating. That can happen to pigs when they go under general anesthesia. Sometimes there's nothing you can do to bring the temperature back down. And there has been very little research and scant knowledge about why this condition happens or how to know if the animal is at risk for it.

This is it, I thought. *This is how they're gonna kill her*. I pleaded with the doctor to try the X-rays without sedating her. At this point they were still just trying to figure out what the problem was. I knew they would need to sedate her if they found she needed surgery, and at that point, we'd accept the associated risks of sedation because it would be necessary. But I couldn't stand the thought of taking the risk for a simple X-ray. Unfortunately, Esther had been a bit snappy during her initial examination, so despite my pleading, the doctor wasn't willing to do the X-rays if she wasn't sedated.

The doctor started rattling off reasons she had to be sedated. His tone was progressing from slightly annoyed to downright fed up. I could tell I was losing the battle, so I played my final card. I had been holding back tears since we first arrived, and I finally just gave in and let them go. I literally burst into tears like I had lost the love of my life. I'm talking full-on wailing.

"Just give me a few minutes to try," I sobbed. "If I can't get what you need, we'll do it your way, no questions asked. Just let me try." The doctor looked a bit taken aback. I'm sure he didn't know what to make of the whole situation. Let's be honest, this had to be the first time he'd ever seen a grown man erupt into borderline hysteria, sobbing and begging, because he didn't want a pig sedated. For a few seconds, he looked like he wanted to object, but I think he realized this was no everyday pig, and this wasn't going to be a normal case by any means. He finally said, "You've got twenty minutes." Then he turned and walked away with the rest of the medical team.

A few minutes later, the X-ray technician showed up with a lead vest and a handheld machine that looked like a big two-handled Polaroid camera. It came with square cartridges that held the film. I had to place the film behind Esther's leg, then get her to hold still long enough for me to grab the camera thingy and take the picture. This wasn't just a matter of "put in the film and snap a quick photo." They needed multiple angles, and the film had to be placed in the perfect position, or it wouldn't capture the image they needed. Esther was restless, but she had been given pain medication, so I knew she was feeling at least a little bit better.

I tried using foam wedges to hold the film at the proper angle. I'd get it all jimmied in place just perfectly, grab the camera, get ready to take the X-ray . . . and then Esther would adjust her leg and knock it all over. It seemed like another losing battle, and I had wasted almost half of the film cartridges they brought me, without getting a single usable picture.

Derek was the only other person who could come into her stall without Esther's getting all paranoid that she'd be jabbed with yet another needle. So he was trying to keep her distracted while I gave it one last attempt. I laid down the foam wedge and placed the film on top of it. Then, ever so slowly, I slid her leg up onto the film without having to lift it at all. I grabbed the camera and got my first successful shot. Finally! I repositioned everything to try for the next few angles, and although I did waste a few more film cartridges, I eventually managed to get clear shots of every angle they needed. And I did it without any sedation—for Esther, I mean. For all I know, the doctor stuck me in the neck with something really quickly to calm me down. (Not really, of course, but I probably could've used it.)

So that all went well. One little victory.

And then we got the bad news.

The X-ray results confirmed our worst fears. Esther had developed an abscess in one of her toes, and it was dangerously close to what they actually call the coffin joint. No kidding.

Like, really? I'm supposed to remain calm when the very joint with a problem just happens to be named after a casket? Not ominous at all!

At that point, it was already well into the evening, and both Derek and I were exhausted. The vet tech told us if the infection got into the bone, it could be a life-threatening situation. The only option was surgery, which they scheduled for the next morning.

In other words, Esther would have to sleep there that night.

That's when I remembered the rules Dr. Kirkham had sternly conveyed from the hospital: no photos, no guests... I was weighing everything in my mind. How much of a pain did I want to be on our first night here? Did I really want to piss off these doctors before they put my baby under the knife?

Derek and I were sitting on the floor in the stall with Esther, trying to comfort her after what had been just as stressful a day for her. The stall itself was about ten feet by twelve feet, with cinderblock walls about six feet high, and solid concrete floors padded with pine shavings over rubber mats. It looked like the stalls were set up mainly for horses or cows, because there were little metal hay feeders in the corner and heavy metal gates at the front that looked like they could contain a rhino. There was a row of about six stalls on one side and a "milking rack" on the other. Apparently they would bring in dairy cows and use them to train students on using the equipment, examining animals, doing various tests, and so on. It was a stark reminder of what kind of facility we were in.

I was glad all the other stalls and milking racks were empty. It was just the three of us in this section, and Derek and I finally had a moment alone to take a breath and wrap our heads around what was happening. I was lying next to Esther; Derek was sitting beside us, talking on the phone to check in with our farm sitters back at the property. He told them we were just going to stay with Esther for a few more minutes, that we'd head home soon and come back to OVC first thing in the morning for the surgery. As I listened to him, all I could think was, *No.* I was looking around at the milking racks across the hall and picturing Esther sitting here all alone, scared and in pain. There was no way in hell I was leaving.

Derek hung up the phone. Before I could even open my mouth, he said, "Are you gonna come home, or do you want to try to stay here?" He knows me better than anyone, so of course he knew I desperately wanted to stay. But we'd already talked about not pushing the boundaries too far, especially after my little breakdown earlier with the X-rays.

Ultimately, we decided we wouldn't push it on the first night. Esther was sleeping comfortably, and we knew nothing was going to happen until morning. I could go home tonight and come back first thing, like 7 a.m. first thing, which you know is early for me. Even if that meant sitting around in the facility for hours with Esther before the doctor arrived.

As Derek and I were just about to pack up, the X-ray tech came in and handed me a piece of paper. "Here's the Wi-Fi password," she said, smiling. "You might get bored tonight without it." Turns out we weren't the only ones who knew I didn't want to leave, and someone there understood.

And so began my nine-day stay—yes, you read that correctly—at the Hotel OVC. Derek gave Esther and me a hug and kiss goodbye, and then he went back to the farm and the rest of our fur family, while Esther and I settled in to watch something on Netflix and try to get some sleep before the big day tomorrow.

The following morning was surprisingly calm. I had managed to get some sleep, and Esther didn't move at all during the night, so I had to assume she did as well. She woke up around 8:30 but didn't even try to stand up. She had a big sign on the front of her stall that said NO FOOD, but I did my best to make sure she didn't see it. Derek arrived at 9, and the vet tech and doctors started shuffling in shortly after that. Her procedure would be later that morning, so we hung out with Esther in the stall, watched some more Netflix, and waited.

When the team of doctors and anesthesiologists arrived, Esther could tell something was up and started to get a bit fussy. She would watch everybody, and the minute someone opened the stall door or came too close, she would grunt and start to squirm a bit. The doctor finally came in to start the sedation process, which began with a nasal mist we administered to her ourselves. Esther trusted us, but there's no way she was going to let the doctor put a syringe up her nose.

Step one went really well. The grunting slowed, and her reaction to people entering the stall all but stopped. It seemed like a good time to administer the needle that would take her sedation to the next level and allow them to insert a catheter into her ear for the general anesthesia. The doctor prepared the needle and went behind Esther so he could stick her in the butt. He got the needle in, but before he could depress the plunger to administer the drug, Esther came to life and shot up like a freight train. The needle remained in, but it was hanging off her butt while she paced and squealed at the gate to get out. My calm state went right out the window as panic once again set in. The doctor managed to get ahold of the syringe and inject the medication, but Esther wasn't going down easily; her adrenaline was too high, and she fought the effects of the medication. It took about twenty minutes for her to finally lie down, which she did with her snout against the gate.

The whole experience was so sad, and it did nothing to make me feel any better about what was going on. The hardest thing with animals is knowing they don't understand what's going on, and there's no way to communicate with them that you're doing something to help them. She was so scared, and we knew all she wanted to do was run away. We knew this was for her own good; she had no idea. All we could do was try our best to comfort her and each other. When she was finally down and the doctors got the catheter in, Derek and I took a quick walk to get some air and let the doctors do their thing.

When we returned a few minutes later, they were already well underway with the surgery, clearing the infection from Esther's hoof. They drilled out the bottom of the hoof, all the way up to the bones in her knuckles. They also inserted a port above her ankle to let any fluids drain out.

They cleaned the area, then packed it with gauze and taped it all up. The procedure itself was very straightforward and didn't take more than an hour. Despite how traumatic this situation was, the procedure went smoothly, and we were thankful for that.

Esther's waking up after surgery, however, was a whole different story.

At first, the process was going according to plan. By 2 p.m. she was opening her eyes and starting to move her legs. She'd yawn and move her tongue around, licking her lips. Everything seemed fine, so much so that Derek went back to the farm for a bit. I was just sitting on the floor in the stall beside Esther, talking to her, making sure she knew I was there. A few hours passed, and all was relatively peaceful given the events of the past twenty-four hours.

Then everything went to hell.

It was around dinnertime. Esther suddenly started panting. Her breathing was labored, and she started frantically moving her legs as if she were running in place. It seemed she was panicking, and it scared the shit out of me. I was afraid it was hyperthermia. It can be deadly, and sometimes once it starts, it can't be stopped. I screamed for the vet techs. I ran to the end of the hall and grabbed the first person I saw. I explained to her what was happening, and she raced off toward another wing of the hospital to get someone else.

When I got back to Esther, she already looked worse. I could feel her skin getting warm to the touch, and she looked flushed all over. Her breathing was more rapid, and her mouth was wide open. Two vet techs came running in with rubbing alcohol and started dumping it all over her. They opened the outside door to bring down the temperature of the ward and brought in two big box fans, pointing them at her. They placed others around the stall to keep the air circulating.

I know I've said this type of thing before, but this time I mean it: these were honestly the scariest few hours of my life. I had heard so many horror stories from other people about what can happen with pigs in surgery, and I thought Esther's was becoming one of those stories.

This whole awful experience went on for close to five hours, until about 10 p.m., when she finally started returning to normal. She had rubbed the skin clean off her knees and the front of her feet from running in place. We hadn't even noticed that happening in all of the chaos. Poor Esther looked like she had been to hell and back.

Thankfully, things got better from there. She was finally out of the woods. (That's ironic for a pig who likes nothing more than to be in the woods, which is a joke I can make only in retrospect.)

Over the next seven days, Esther's condition steadily improved. It turned out that the medications she had been given had built up in the fat in her body, taking much longer to leave her system than medication does in leaner animals. It's yet another reason why maintaining a healthy weight is so important for pigs. Being even slightly overweight can cause not only joint and muscle issues but also very dangerous reactions during (and following) medical procedures.

We found out that people had been calling the hospital and sending gifts for Esther, a practice that obviously isn't common at a large animal hospital. The administrators also decided to keep Esther in the private ward, so no one else could get in to see her. It also allowed us to let her out of her stall after a couple of days, so she could explore and stretch her legs.

It was really funny because she refused to go to the bathroom in her stall. She would stand at her gate until you opened it, then walk to the opposite end of the ward before doing her business, just like she wouldn't go to the bathroom in our home. She took over that space like it was hers, and the hospital staffers were totally cool with it. The more time I spent there, the more I got to speak with all the staff at the facility. It was an amazingly eye-opening experience. They let me ask a whole bunch of questions, and I learned a lot from them. And in the process, I think they learned a lot about my experiences and perspective. They were truly great with us, especially with me and all my needs when it came to being near my girl. If I didn't say it enough then, I should say a big thank-you right here to the doctors and all the staff at OVC who helped save our amazing pig-daughter.

It hadn't been our intention to make waves, but I know our time there was memorable for the staff at OVC. We've even been told they will be adding a course for the care of large companion animals like Esther, something they never offered in the past. While I can't say for sure that we influenced their decision, I'd like to think we played a small part in helping them see things a little differently.

Most of the time in large animal clinics, the owners just leave the animal, and it's usually something like a horse or a show cow. It's not very often somebody spends thousands of dollars on a pig, let alone refuses to leave the animal's side. Nobody would think twice about it if she were a dog—my actions would have been seen as nothing more than those of a concerned parent. But because the patient was a commercial pig, they simply weren't prepared for the reaction they got, and at least a few of the staff members said goodbye to Esther and us with a much different outlook than they'd had when we arrived.

CHAPTER EIGHT

After nine long days in the hospital, bringing Esther home was such a relief. We knew she would need a few weeks of taking it easy before she'd be fully back to her regular routine. We were just happy she was home, and I was more than ready to sleep in my bed, instead of on pine shavings.

What Derek and I didn't expect were all the little behavioral changes that started creeping up almost immediately upon her return. Her personality was much softer. Those little anger flashes and the bratty attitude, particularly toward Derek, had subsided. She was much calmer and sweeter than she had been. She started sitting up in bed during the day and would hang her head while simultaneously making little honking noises. She had done that before on occasion, usually during Shark Week (which is what we call her period), and we had a whole routine when that happened: Either Derek or I would stop what we were doing and go over and sit beside her. That was usually all she wanted. Once you were there, she would lie back down while you sat with her for a few minutes. Then you could get up and go back to what you were doing. Now, however, she was hanging her head and making the noises much more frequently. And as soon as you got up to go, she'd get up too. She wanted somebody beside her at all times, and the dogs weren't good enough. It had to be one of us.

She even started coming into the bedroom at night, giving us flashbacks to our time in Georgetown and the "piggy parades." We'd hear her coming down the hallway and know she was heading straight for our bed. We'd quickly get our dog Shelby out of the way and brace for Esther's arrival, at which point she'd storm right onto the bed. The funniest part was that she always climbed up on Derek's side. (Well, funny for me, less funny for Derek.) She'd grunt as she approached, but she didn't slow down one bit as she lumbered onto the mattress, pushing Derek out so she could lie down with me. This happened every night for two weeks, until we finally accepted defeat. We moved upstairs to the guest room, surrendering the master bedroom to Esther.

This coincided with our finally starting to do some renovations on the house, particularly to what was now Esther's bedroom. The original wallpaper was right out of the eighties: a white background with a raised floral pattern and metallic accents in pink and silver. Once, it might have been quite fashionable, but that time was a few decades ago, before we were even born. Acid-washed jeans and overalls apparently were fashionable back then as well, but that didn't mean we wanted them in our home.

The paper was also starting to peel—almost the entire sheet in certain places. We had used box tape as a temporary fix to hold it in place until we got around to renovating. Needless to say, the room looked superchic—even more so once we removed some of the bedroom furniture, which had been strategically placed to hide some rougher-looking sections of the wall. And did I mention the beige broadloom? I'm sure you can imagine what it looked like after a few months of muddy puppy paws and pig hooves. Like most of the house (or virtually any house, if I'm being honest), it really wasn't designed for an unconventional family such as ours. We just didn't know where to start. It was like trying to figure out triage after a disaster: everything looked like it needed to be fixed immediately.

Actually, we had lived with this décor for a year—we'd just dealt with it. Sure, it was unsightly, but whatever. We'd had so many other priorities to handle. I'm kind of amazed we let it go as long as we did. And now, Esther had been in the bedroom for two weeks and the princess already had a cosmetic crew to glam it up!

Until Esther moved in, we didn't photograph that room—or at least share the photos on our social media—very often. If we did, we tried to present it as nicely as possible, like how someone who takes a lot of selfies for Instagram seems to take shots from only the most flattering angle. (Is there really only one side to your face? What are you, the Phantom of the Opera?) I'd take photos of the room from only certain angles, to avoid showing a damaged portion of the wall or how our mattress sat right on the floor, as if we were in our first apartment and couldn't afford a bed frame. (Actually, we put the mattress on the floor so Esther could get up there easily without hurting herself.)

But people on the internet can be really judgmental, so I tried not to show anything that would let somebody say, "See, she's a pig. She belongs in a barn." I also never wanted to give the impression she was dirty or unmanageable. At this point, hundreds of thousands of people were looking into our house on a weekly basis through our posts on the internet, and I didn't want them thinking we lived in squalor, or that Esther was destroying the house. We were trying to improve people's perception of pigs, and essentially living in a pigpen wasn't going to help us do that. We already had done quite a lot to clean things up cosmetically in the main rooms of the house, but our bedroom had remained fairly private, to a certain degree. If it was to become Esther's bedroom and she'd be spending more time in there, I had no choice but to make it Facebook-friendly by giving it a face-lift.

We saved a panel of the hideous wallpaper to cut and frame. One of Esther's fans actually suggested selling pieces of the wallpaper, but we thought that was a bit strange. Who wants a piece of their bedroom hanging in other people's homes? And who wants a piece of someone else's wallpaper? I know they all thought of it as "Esther's bedroom," but even Esther made it clear how much she disliked that paper. At the end of the day, that was our bedroom. That paper had seen me naked. I didn't want it hanging in somebody else's house.

One day, while all the rearranging and redecorating was going on, I got a phone call from a longtime family friend named Wendy. She and her husband had always taken advantage of me, like when I was a teenager and I'd get a frantic call because Wendy hadn't arranged a babysitter, and guess who needed to fill in? On the rare occasion I said I wasn't available, Wendy would go straight to my mom to lay on a guilt trip, and, three more guesses who ended up rearranging his life to accommodate them. It got even worse once I got into real estate. They were the kind of people who expected everyone to bend over backward for them but who would push you aside in a flash if something came along that was more beneficial to them—no matter who was hurt in the process. The last time we had worked together, I ended up reducing my commission by over half to help them get the house they wanted. My belief at the time was that I could sell their current house and make up the money on that end. Everybody thinks real estate agents make tons of money, but by the time we pay our board fees, office fees, insurance, advertising, taxes, and on and on . . . giving someone a 50 percent commission discount basically leaves you with nothing.

I'd given them that huge reduction only because of the

arrangement we had made regarding the sale of their house. But as we've seen before, I tend to be a bit too trusting of people. I trusted their word, but not a week later, I found out they had sold their house with another agent. I was furious, having been through hell and back to get them the new house, only to be totally screwed by these people at their first opportunity.

Anyway, I hadn't heard from them since that debacle. Even my mom had started to distance herself from their family after witnessing how selfish they'd become. Now I was busy with the sanctuary and the renovations. When my phone rang and I saw that it was Wendy, I was actually looking forward to being able to tell her I wasn't working as a Realtor anymore. That wasn't entirely true; I still worked for friends and family. But I sure as hell didn't need to put myself through the hassle of working with clients like Wendy and her husband now.

When I answered, Wendy was her typical sunny self: "It's so good to speak with you. Congratulations on the farm; we'd love to see it." The usual stuff. We chatted for a minute or two about nothing in particular, and then she casually brought up the real reason for her call: "Oh, by the way, we've got this rabbit; can you take it?"

There it was.

I knew there must be a reason she was calling, because in the many years I'd known Wendy, not once did I receive a "Hey, how are you?" kind of phone call. She always had an ulterior motive, and in this case, she had a rabbit to rid herself of.

"It's living in my garage," she said. "We got it for the kids, but they don't care. I'm the only one who loves it."

She threw out every excuse under the sun in a matter of seconds.

I was doing my best to explain that we didn't have a facility yet to take in rabbits. We had only a few hutches, and that was where Derek's rabbits from his former magic act were staying. There were plans to build a space for rabbits eventually, but we hadn't gotten there yet. We had this awesome space right behind the barn earmarked for what we would call Bunny Town. It had existing stone walls on three sides, and the ground was rocky with big trees that provided plenty of shade. It would be ideal for rabbits. They love to dig, so having rocky ground was perfect, because it would help prevent them from digging out under the fences. We were going to put all the individual hutches within this fenced-in area and bring in topsoil so we could plant grass for them to graze on.

But those were plans for the future. At the moment when Wendy was calling, the whole space was still filled with garbage. There was even a mattress with a tree growing through it (don't ask) and, of course, plenty of broken glass.

I was in the middle of a sentence, trying to explain this to Wendy, when suddenly her husband, Walter, came on the phone and said, "Hey, Stevie boy! I hear you're taking the rabbit! That's great, we'll see you soon!" and hung up.

He didn't even give me time to answer, probably sensing that my conversation with Wendy wasn't going too well. They needed to get rid of the rabbit, and they didn't care how it happened. I stood there with the phone still in my hand for a moment as I replayed that last part and the fact that, apparently, we were about to get a rabbit dumped on us.

My first thought was to go tell Derek, but he already hated Wendy and Walter due to the history we shared together, so I knew it wouldn't be pretty. But part of me thought, *There's no way she's that thoughtless.* I figured she would have smacked Walter in the arm when he hung up. She would have told him they weren't showing up with a rabbit based on the conversation we'd just had, one in which I never even agreed to take the rabbit—or even had a chance to respond.

Turns out I was right: They didn't show up. They made one of their friends do it.

You see, the only reason Wendy even thought to call me was because of a blanket drive for the sanctuary that happened to be organized by a friend of hers. She didn't make the connection at first, until this lady arrived to pick up Wendy's contribution of blankets. They got to chatting, and that's when Wendy realized I was the one who had the sanctuary. Wendy saw an opportunity to add a little something to her donation. She presented it to this poor lady as if it were all arranged, as though we were eagerly awaiting the arrival of this adorable little bunny rabbit. The liar.

Derek and I saw Wendy's friend pull up; it had been only

a few hours since Wendy's phone call. Knowing the woman was arriving with a load of blankets, we both went out to meet her. But she obviously saw us coming, and before we even got to the gate, she leaned out the window of her minivan and cheerfully exclaimed, "I'm here with your new bunny!"

Derek laughed, assuming she was joking. He made some smart-ass retort like "Awesome, I hope you brought lots of bunnies. And I hope they're washed and folded, because the big ones are a real pain to get into our little washing machine." It was a comedy of errors, because they both thought the other was in on the joke. But I immediately started to put the pieces together and knew she was dead serious about the bunny. I proceeded to walk—very quickly I might add—toward the barn, while Derek closed the gate and came up behind us. Wendy's friend was already out of the car and at the passenger door by the time we caught up with her.

"Hi, I'm Sandra," she said as we approached. "And this is Tulip."

She lifted a little cat carrier off the seat, a huge smile flashing on her face. She was so excited to be delivering Tulip to her new home, and she had no idea we weren't expecting this new resident. Hell, Derek didn't even know about the phone call a couple of hours earlier, let alone that the phone call had ended with the possibility of a rabbit's coming to live with us. I spoke up right away.

"Oh, this is the rabbit. Perfect."

I was hoping to avoid an awkward confrontation between Derek and Sandra, because it wasn't Sandra's fault in the least, but it was too late. Derek, rightfully, launched into question mode: "When did this happen? Why didn't I know about this?"

Luckily, Derek's wrath was directed entirely toward me, but it was still awkward for Sandra. She stood there like a deer in the headlights, not really sure what to do with herself... or Tulip.

While this particular situation was rather unusual, the phenomenon itself was nothing new. Sanctuaries regularly deal with animals being abandoned at their doors. We'd been warned to prepare ourselves for the day we'd walk outside and find an extra horse just hanging out in our yard. Horses are commonly abandoned, because they can be so expensive to care for. You know the old idiom "eats like a horse." Like most idioms, it exists for a reason.

In addition to all the food, there's medical care, which is virtually extortionate when dealing with horses. It's like comparing a birthday cake and a wedding cake. You can get a slab cake at your local bakery for $20, but if you tell the baker it will be a wedding cake, all of a sudden it's $120. That's kind of how vet care for large animals works. Surgery on a pig? Not too big of a deal, depending on the seriousness of the matter, of course. Surgery on a horse? There's a chance you'll need to remortgage your house.

Surprise arrivals at farm sanctuaries aren't limited to farm animals. Even dogs and cats are regularly found tied to gates or in carriers left at the end of driveways. Obviously this can be a huge problem for a struggling facility.

When an animal arrives at a sanctuary, many things need to happen. First, the animal gets quarantined to make sure it isn't sick and won't pass on some illness to the animals already living at the farm. You need to feed the animal and provide it with its own stall or pasture space until it can be integrated with the other animals. All of this costs time and money—and sometimes, more importantly, space. It immediately diminishes your ability to help another animal that needs you.

Emergencies often come up where there's an animal in immediate peril, but if you're struggling already and dealing with an abandoned horse that arrived the day before, there's nothing you can do. Taking in that additional animal could put your entire farm at risk. The bank doesn't care if your big heart and your even bigger vet bill mean you can't pay the mortgage this month. Some places are literally one animal away from not being able to pay their bills, and very few have cash in the bank at the end of the year. These sanctuaries are calculating where every dollar goes, while trying their best to be prepared for the never-ending surprise expenses that come along with caring for animals.

So when people abandon an animal in this way, they're saddling their responsibilities on others, all because they can't be bothered to do the right thing. Taking an animal into your family is a lifelong commitment, so there really shouldn't be very many instances of people needing to get rid of the animal. That's just selfishness.

When we hear "We're moving and we can't take him/her with us," we're like, *Okay, maybe you'd dump the in-laws, but you'd never leave your children behind*. Animals are children to me, so I just can't wrap my head around that excuse. Thank goodness Derek handles all the intake requests for our sanctuary, because some of the emails he shows me make my head want to explode.

Occasionally situations arise in which there really is no alternative, such as terminal illness or financial hardships that put your family—both humans and animals—at risk. I get that. Sometimes it really is better for the animal if people give it up. But 99 percent of the time, it's just people being shitty.

So Derek was upset at Tulip's arrival. Poor Sandra had no idea her special present from Wendy was only half-expected (at best) by me and a complete shock to Derek, and she left quickly to escape the awkwardness. Once she was gone, things only got more tense.

Derek was furious, assuming I was totally in on the plan to bring a bunny home. While I'd had an idea a rabbit might show up, I wasn't sure, and I certainly didn't expect it to show up within an hour of Walter's abruptly hanging up on me. Sure, I've screwed up before by not keeping Derek in the loop on everything, but this time, I hadn't had a chance to do the right thing! I'd assumed Wendy would call me back to nail down the details. (Of course, now I know never to give Wendy the benefit of the doubt.)

I explained the phone-call situation to Derek, but I'm pretty sure he still thought I was more complicit in the Tulip situation than I actually was. In the past, when Derek had listened to me vent about Wendy and Walter, I'd always defended her. So he thought this was just another example of my being a pushover. It took a lot of convincing to get him to believe I was as taken aback as he was.

Ultimately, it turned out to be less of an imposition than it originally seemed. It wasn't as if Sandra had just dropped off a herd of cows; one rabbit wasn't going to bankrupt our farm. However, I realized I needed to be more firm when discussing important farm matters with people, because they don't impact only me; they affect Derek just as much, and depending on the situation, a bit of confusion could create major problems for the sanctuary itself.

But that's hard. I'm a softy. Flat-out saying no has always been hard for me. Most of the time, I'll inconvenience myself no end before I'll inconvenience someone else—and yes, that includes even someone who's been as, um, selfish at times as Wendy. Sometimes you just need to be a big boy and firmly say no, and that's what I should have done with Wendy. I'm still working on developing that skill. But again, this was just a rabbit—our first experience with what was essentially an abandoned animal, and we knew it wouldn't be our last.

We had a spare hutch for Tulip to live in, but it wasn't very big, and given that we already had the vision for Bunny Town in our minds, we decided we needed to move it up on the priority list. Just as Esther inspired our bedroom renovation, Tulip inspired the construction of Bunny Town. We got to work on cleaning out the trash and repairing the stone walls.

Most of it was really straightforward work. But the rabbits also needed overhead protection, to keep them safe from birds of prey and other potential dangers from above. That's something we hadn't dealt with before, and we'd never done any sort of construction on such a large scale. The pen was massive, with enormous old maple trees and dozens of smaller saplings. We didn't want to cut anything down, because it was so perfect for the rabbits. Having a natural environment for them was the whole reason we were building this pen, so cutting down all the trees wasn't an option. We'd need a work-around.

We decided to get huge batting cage nets and stitch them together with hundreds of zip ties to make a single net large enough to cover the entire enclosure. We went up and over the smaller trees, then cut around the big trees so they'd extend out above the nets. The result was a 100 percent enclosed, supercool, supersafe space for our rabbit family to explore. Perfect, right?

We thought so, but the Bunny Police did not. And believe me, the Vegan Police are pussycats compared to the Bunny Police. They believe (and insist) that domestic rabbits should live only indoors. Never outdoors. The hate campaigns that sprang up from the moment we announced the completion of Bunny Town were astonishing. We'd even get emails that would start out asking questions about the enclosure and being all sweet and nice. We'd be pleasant in return. We'd explain why we built an outdoor enclosure, the extra steps we'd taken to ensure the rabbits were protected during bad weather and from predators, to ensure they received health care, and so on. We covered all our bases, having consulted both with our vet and with other sanctuaries to find out what they did. Some gave awesome advice, while others said they didn't "do bunnies" anymore, because it was too controversial.

They weren't kidding. We'd had no idea how controversial our bunny enclosure would be, and the battles went on for weeks. The critics were ruthless, saying we were unfit to run a sanctuary because we were idiots. I very rarely get blocked on social media—other than by Rosie O'Donnell, for reasons I still don't understand. (Maybe she'll call us one day, and we can resolve our differences with a Koosh ball battle.) But I've been blocked by members of the Vegan Police and the Bunny Police. We're always dealing with the odd message complaining about one thing or another.

Blah, blah, blah.

No matter what you do, someone always has a problem

with it. Bunny Town was no different. People would come in, guns blazing, saying we were putting the rabbits at risk. As far as these people were concerned, rabbits belonged indoors, and under no circumstances should they be allowed to live outside. Yet I'm pretty sure these are the same animals I see in our forest, or happily hopping through our pastures, on a daily basis. I could not understand how their instincts to explore and be outdoors would have disappeared because of domestication.

Dogs still have a pack mentality, cats still hunt mice despite having plenty of food to eat at home, and rabbits still enjoy grassy meadows and forests. As far as we're concerned, our job as a sanctuary is to provide our animal residents with the best, most natural life possible. And we don't believe any animal deserves to spend its life locked indoors.

CHAPTER NINE

By the time our first spring rolled around, we were finally getting into the groove of things as far as country life was concerned. I couldn't wait for the winter weather to break and to finally let the fire go out in the house—it had been going around the clock all winter. When we first got to the farm, I thought having a wood-burning stove would be amazing. We had tons of land with tons of wood, so it seemed perfect. We could heat our home for free all winter!

Yeah... that was just another thing we couldn't have been more wrong about. Sure, there's more wood on the property than we could ever burn. But the idea that it would be free failed to factor in the process of turning a tree into fuel: getting the firewood out of the forest, chopping it up into manageable pieces, stacking it to let it properly dry, and then finally bringing it into the house is a lot of work. And I'm not saying that because we actually did it. We were clever enough to figure out that we wouldn't be able to do it ourselves once we started to think about how to make it happen.

Despite the enormous resources outside our door, honestly, we ended up ordering the vast majority of our firewood. And it was superexpensive—not because of the cost of the wood itself, but because of the amount we used. We went through more than nineteen face cords of wood. Don't worry, I won't bore you with the details, but you could basically build a four-foot-high solid log fence around the typical suburban property with the amount we used. It was madness. It came stacked on pallets that we had dropped off beside our driveway. We'd move it from there to our front deck, and then into the dining room, where the woodstove was. Every single piece was moved by hand, multiple times. Needless to say, the novelty of that cozy stove wore off really quickly.

The other thing I was really looking forward to with spring was that we would finally be able to make some serious progress on the property. We had used the winter to get ourselves settled, and we'd slowly started bringing in extra hands to help. But spring and summer would see our official grand opening and tour days, along with volunteers arriving to clear pastures, build fences, and clean up the farm. Our plans were about to start coming together really quickly, and the closer we got to that first collective workday, the more nervous we became.

Before we moved, Derek and I had worked together, but it was really just the two of us, plus maybe one other person who helped with bookkeeping or my real estate paperwork. I'm an idea person, not a paperwork person. The transition to the farm had been amazing, but now we found ourselves awaiting the arrival of literally thousands of people over the course of the summer, and we had no idea what to do with them. Managing yourself is easy enough. It takes discipline, but it's not rocket science. Managing large teams of people of various backgrounds and skill sets—that's an entirely different ball game.

We also had to start planning the tour aspect of the sanctuary schedule. We barely knew our way around the farm ourselves—it felt like everywhere we looked, the final layout remained just an idea waiting to come to fruition. There was still so much more to do. So what were we going to show everybody? What were we going to say?

We tried to come up with a very simple itinerary for visitors. It would include the barn, a walk through the woods, and the old farm road, which serviced the other fifty acres of our farm. The farm had once been a one-hundred-acre property, but sadly, it had been divided before we purchased it. Either way, the old road was still there, so we figured the tour would use that to get to our back property line and then would cut across the top of the pasture behind our barn, and finally go down the middle to where it started. It covered only about 20 percent of the property, but at least it was a start. That said, actually using the farm road remained just an idea at that stage. It hadn't been used in decades, so it had basically reverted to being part of the forest again. Clearing it became one of the first projects we would do on Get Dirty Day, the first official, public event at the sanctuary.

Get Dirty Day was a perk we created during the Indiegogo crowdfunding campaign. It offered Esther's fans the opportunity to join us for the very first public workday at the farm. We had more than a hundred people registered to join us, with some arriving from as far away as Australia, to help get the farm ready for opening day in July.

Derek and I always knew it was a must to be cautious around the animals. Everyone has heard horror stories about people being injured while working with large animals. In fact, we'd had a visit from the manager of one of the most renowned farm sanctuaries in the world, and she told us a story about how her favorite cow—they were best friends, she said—almost killed her one night in the barn when the cow lost her mind about something and freaked out. Luckily, the manager was able to slip out between the fence boards; she narrowly escaped without injury. But this was coming from someone who literally could write the book on caring for farm animals. I believe she knows more than most people who teach at vet schools. So if something like that can happen to her, it can happen to anyone, with any animal.

Similarly, we had our fair share of animals with attitude, so we knew we'd need to watch them quite closely as the number of people coming through the property started to increase. A particular one to watch was Diablo the goat. He had come to us after a zoo had a fire in its barn exhibit and the managers decided not to rebuild. That left all their farm animals without a home. They contacted us, and we agreed to bring in three goats, two sheep, and two Flemish giant rabbits. The rabbits moved to Bunny Town, while the goats and sheep joined our existing goat family. Diablo got on fine with all of his pasture-mates, but he wasn't a big fan of people. He would act all cuddly and rub up against you, and then he'd whip his head back and try to impale you with his formidable horns. They're about twelve inches long, curving downward toward his back, and both are sharp enough to be very intimidating, especially because they're attached to a two-hundred-pound goat.

All the animals have characters and personalities; you just need to learn what to look for. I love Diablo, and I often go into his pasture for a wrestling match. I swear he loves to play, but you can tell when he goes from having friendly fun to fuming and being ready to actually hurt you. He's like a lot of house cats that way. One second, the sweet kitty is contentedly purring away; the next, she's trying to flay the skin off your forearm with her claws. Not so worrisome with a small house cat, but imagine if Furry McFurryface suddenly transformed into a mountain lion.

A few months after Diablo and his friends arrived, we got a call for two other sheep that had been found in a "dead pile" at the end of a farmer's driveway not far from where we live. In other words, a passerby noticed some movement within a pile of other babies that weren't so lucky. She stopped immediately, found these two babies, put them in her car, and took them home to be rehabilitated. Seeing them now, it's hard to believe they were ever discarded as waste. Their names are Moose and Yammy. They're both nearly black, with almost silver streaks in their wool, like salt-and-pepper hair. They are two of the sweetest sheep we've ever met. Moose, in particular, loves affection and attention; he's always coming up to people when they enter his field. He's by far the most social of all our sheep, and his is one of the only pastures we could let people into without being nervous that someone might get hurt.

At least, that seemed to be the case.

One day we had a tour group going through, and out of nowhere, Moose decided anyone under about four feet tall was not welcome in his pasture. He approached a little girl and sniffed her, just looking all cute as he always does. Then he casually took a few steps back. And then he rammed her!

I'm a terrible person, so my immediate instinct was to laugh hysterically, although I did simultaneously run over to make sure the girl was okay. Fortunately for me, some-one else was laughing even harder, and it was the little girl's mother, who had realized her daughter was totally fine, if a bit embarrassed. After the ramming, Moose just casually wandered off as if nothing had happened. It blew my mind. Sweet, gentle Moose could be a linebacker for the Buffalo Bills? Who knew?

And this wasn't a one-time occurrence. It has since hap-pened a number of times, always with small children. We're trying to figure out if it's a girl or a boy thing, but Moose doesn't seem to care about that. When he sees a child, he just rams full-tilt. Which is funny to witness, but not so enjoyable for the small person. Moose is normally a very sweet sheep who always comes up to the fence and wants to be petted. But he's got no tolerance for short people. So far, the only common denominator we've found is height, so if you're under four feet tall and plan to visit, you'll want to stay clear of Moose.

We also have a rooster named Davey Cockett, and there's no point in trying to sugarcoat it: He's a jerk. Davey hates everyone. He will chase you and not stop, often going on for much longer than you ever anticipated running. Just when you think he's gone and you slow down...you find out he's right on your heels. I'm not ashamed to admit that I am more afraid of the roosters than any of the other animals on our farm. I'd rather run from a pig any day, because roosters are like tiny ninjas with feathers, and they're on you before you even know what's happening. They jump up and use their legs to kick you a thousand times in the span of a half second. Their whole objective is to stab you with their little claws (called spurs) on the back of their legs, and it hurts like a bugger when they get you. It's literally a blur. I pretty much live in fear of Davey Cockett. As we learn every animal's personality, we discover not only how to deal with them but also which ones can and can't be allowed to greet our guests on open days.

When Get Dirty Day was just around the corner, the excitement was really building. I couldn't wait to finally get some of the bigger projects we had planned underway. Looking at the aerial photo of the farm, walking around, and making plans is fun. But there's nothing quite like actually seeing those plans start to come together. We spent all winter coming up with ideas and deciding what to do first. All the imagining and plotting was enjoyable, but I was ready to amp things up the way we knew only a hundred pairs of hands could do. Plus, we'd have a few extra volunteers on hand to help, as well as the board of directors. Derek and I had planned the day as best we could. We made a list of projects we wanted to tackle and were feeling good about everything as the time neared. We also had been hyping it online.

It had been only a few months since we'd moved to the farm, but it felt for us as if a lifetime had gone by. The whirlwind hadn't calmed down at all, and our online supporters were just as excited as we were to see us really get down to work. Then, before we knew it, it was the night before Get Dirty Day.

It had been just over two years since we'd started the Facebook page, and some of the Get Dirty participants had been following our adventure from the very beginning. But this would be the first time most of them met Esther in person, the first time they didn't need to rely on Facebook to see her.

As cars started to arrive in the morning, the excitement level was through the roof. One of the first people to pull up saw Esther and me walking into our backyard. The woman was so excited, she literally jumped from her car and started running toward us as the car—which was still in Drive—rolled onward. She realized what she had done and stopped for a second, looking first at her car, then at us, before she frantically ran back to the car and slammed it into Park. I nearly died laughing.

Derek had come out of the mobile home just as it was all playing out. He walked over to me with a look of total disbelief on his face. We knew people had developed very meaningful relationships with Esther via her social media pages, but we hadn't realized the level of celebrity status she had garnered with them. She was the Britney Spears of the porcine world, and she could literally move people to tears simply by brushing her snout against their pant legs. Sometimes she'd move me that way too, I must admit, but Esther is my baby. I'd be sitting with her and I'd let my mind wander… and before I knew it, I'd be in tears, thinking about her lost pig family or the things we did before we knew Esther. I'm sure I'll always feel guilty for not going vegan sooner, and I have a feeling that's a big part of why Esther makes others emotional too. She becomes a connection point for people. We've seen in countless messages written to us that even a package of bacon at the grocery store can be enough to bring Esther's image to mind for some people. It's the whole idea of giving food a face and putting a living animal at the front of someone's mind—something that typically gets ignored altogether. I never gave a second thought to what I was seeing at the grocery store before Esther came along; now when

I happen to catch sight of packages of meat, I see nothing but faces.

All morning we watched people get out of their cars with the most incredible looks on their faces when they saw Esther for the first time. Some cried, some laughed, and some stood silently and just watched. It was an amazing experience, and it really drove home the impact Esther was having on other people's lives, not just our own.

We mingled for about an hour before we started rounding everybody up to get working. Then the initial excitement gave way to focused determination to get the job done. Everybody scattered into teams, and we each set off to handle our respective jobs.

Derek and I floated around to oversee everything and make sure we spent a little bit of time with everybody, as hosts are expected to do. We realized almost immediately that work slowed dramatically whenever we got involved, because everybody wanted to chat. To be fair, I'm the worst when it comes to that—I could talk the ear off a dead man, and I'm just as excited to meet everyone else as they are to meet us and, obviously, Esther, who was the main attraction.

One thing we knew we needed was a quarantine pen. We wanted to have a place away from the main barn that could hold new arrivals and also a stall in the garage for emergency medical situations. It had been in the plan since day one, so we wanted to get it up and running ASAP.

Derek and I headed over toward the garage, where a group

of people were cleaning up what would be our new quarantine pen. One of our volunteers—Ted, the guy who makes Esther's T-shirts, in fact—was pulling up an old tree root. Suddenly, the root snapped, and he went tumbling backward, landing hard on one shoulder. For a few moments, we weren't too concerned, because he didn't seem to be hurt. He stood up, looking a little embarrassed—even though he had no reason to be—and played it off as if it were nothing. But then he tried to raise his arm, and that's when we knew it was serious. He'd broken his arm. We were only a few hours into our very first workday, and already we had a broken bone. It wasn't pretty. Ted tried to downplay the injury, but of course we sent him to the hospital.

The injury drove home how large the task as well as the risk we had taken on really were. We'd put everything on the line, and in that moment, we felt like we had no idea what we were doing. We'd never had a serious injury to anyone until this moment. Now we were worried about potentially being sued or found negligent because we really weren't qualified to be operating a farm.

It's not that we hadn't been taking things seriously before, but this was the first time we'd had the general public visit the farm, and that's extremely different from having a bunch of friends over to help you move. Plus, you hear about crazy lawsuits all the time. Didn't somebody sue McDonald's for burning themselves on hot coffee? And win? It's ridiculous what people sue for these days. Considering the situation at the farm, there were so many potential risks. We had people repairing stone walls, pulling out stumps, using tools, and crossing rough terrain. It seemed to me like an ambulance-chasing lawyer's dream. I mean, we didn't think Esther's true fans had any such ulterior motives, but it's not like you can completely vet everyone who offers to volunteer at the farm—for all we knew, there could be a wolf in sheep's clothing somewhere in the mix. We also felt sometimes as if we had an extra target on our backs because of Esther's online presence and what we at Esther the Wonder Pig stand for as an organization.

We've received a few threatening messages since this all began, some scary enough that we called the police. There's no denying that Esther poses a threat to the livelihood of certain people in the animal-agriculture industry. We've even been blocked on Twitter by the Manitoba Pork Council—maybe Rosie O. has a friend there or something—and a few other very large agricultural organizations, including some government-run agencies. I find this crazy. I typically don't engage much with those types of organizations, but I felt I had no choice after a certain situation came up in Manitoba.

In the summer of 2015, a pig escaped from a slaughterhouse and was found wandering the streets. It somehow became a huge news story, and of course the vegan community pleaded for the pig to be released to a sanctuary. Derek and I got involved as well, making phone calls to the appropriate people, including the Manitoba Pork Council, but we were all unsuccessful. The pig, who came to be known as Mercy, was quietly sent to slaughter—even though the authorities told the public that she was receiving medical care. In truth, they never had any intention of letting her live, no matter how hard she fought for her freedom.

Even before Esther came along, I remember seeing stories of animals escaping from slaughterhouses and running around the city. I always found myself cheering them on, as so many people do. I'd be hoping someone would catch them and whisk them off to a safe-forever home where they'd live out their days in some beautiful rolling pasture. But even then, I managed to keep myself from thinking about the ones who didn't escape, or the ones who had no one cheering them on.

But the Mercy situation was different. When they sent Mercy away, I kept engaging on the Manitoba Pork Council's social media pages in a very Esther way. When they'd tweet something advertising pork loin or bacon, I'd post a picture of Esther beside Shelby or one of the cats, along with something rather benign such as "Why love one but eat the other?" I remained gentle. I was never rude or aggressive. But it was enough to rub them the wrong way, so they blocked me from seeing or responding to their tweets. The animal-agriculture industry relies on marketing to keep people feeling good about consuming their products, so the thought of people starting to think about farm animals the same way we think about companion animals must be terrifying for them.

It's that whole situation, along with the messages we got as a result of speaking up so much about it, that really started to concern me about Esther's security. We already walked with her everywhere she went, but the world is a crazy place, and it doesn't take too much time watching the news to know people do some truly senseless things. With so much to be aware of, we knew we had to make sure we covered ourselves. Our insurance adjuster came out to the farm, and we purchased a comprehensive policy on the property—and on ourselves.

As time went on, we hired a staff member to help us keep up with orders from the Esther Store, and additional regular volunteers started to work their way into our daily lives. It was all wonderful, but it took us awhile to get used to it.

Every morning, Derek's favorite thing is to take a quick soak in our hot tub, which helps ease a sore back he's had for years. He also happens to prefer doing this ritual without a bathing suit—not necessarily something our volunteers want to see first thing in the morning (not that I have any complaints). He always says, "It's just a penis, who cares?" And at the end of the day, he's right: they all look more or less the same. But we still couldn't take the chance of offending people, which meant adjusting his hot-tub schedule to make sure he was done by the time people started to arrive. It's a minor detail, but it was one of the first things we needed to change about our life at the sanctuary. Personal time was still personal, but it could be interrupted at any moment.

We also had to make sure we were ready whenever people started to arrive, so we could give them instructions for the day and keep everyone on track. The more people who got involved, the more we started to hear everyone else's thoughts on how things should be done. Having a lot of people around can be a blessing and a curse, both from a management perspective and because you can quickly get into a "too many cooks" situation. Certain helpers would start expressing concerns about a fence or how big the pasture was for B.J. and Escalade. It didn't matter what got done, there was always somebody—usually at one of the public workdays—who thought they knew a better way.

But it wasn't always about what we *did*. Sometimes it was what we *didn't do*.

Take our first barn cat, Catt Damon. (Yes, you have to love puns if you want to love us.) Catt Damon came to us via the local Humane Society, and like the inspiration for his name, he was incredibly handsome: he was a large longhair with silver-and-black fur. He was quite affectionate and took his job as barn manager very seriously. He slept in a little cat hut in the feed room and would poke his little head out as soon as you visited in the morning. His food bowl was right outside his hut, so sometimes he'd just lean out and eat while he was still in bed.

We all loved Catt Damon, but one volunteer, Justin, took a particular fancy to him, and as time went on, he got more and more distraught that Catt was a barn cat. He was upset that we hadn't brought him into the house, and he wasn't subtle about his feelings. Almost every time we saw him, he'd say something passive-aggressive about it. And Justin was not shy in the sass department. He'd walk around with Catt in his arms when he was heading to lunch or he'd just carry him wherever he went after he'd finished his volunteer chores.

Derek and I spoke with Justin about it a few times. We reassured him that Catt Damon had everything he could ever need, including a safe barn where we closed him in every night. It didn't help. On at least one occasion, we found Justin in tears about it. He was a very sensitive man. We tried so hard to reassure him that Catt was all set, but nothing seemed to put his mind at ease, no matter how hard we tried. As far as we were concerned, Catt was safe. He had what I'm sure most cats would consider a badass house. It was huge, he could explore wherever he wanted, and he got attention from people constantly. He was living large.

A few weeks went by, and then one morning we went out to the barn and Catt Damon was nowhere to be found. We searched high and low, shaking cat treats in the woods around the barn. We looked everywhere. We didn't freak out right away, because he had taken himself on a walk once before, and it had been a few hours before we'd found him: he'd gone into the woods and climbed high up in a tree. So this time we thought maybe he'd done the same thing—but a search of the nearby woods brought no signs of Catt Damon.

Later that day, we got an email from Justin. He told us his

schedule had changed and that, unfortunately, he wouldn't be able to volunteer regularly anymore. Pretty coincidental timing. We didn't think much of it until the following morning, when we still hadn't been able to find Catt Damon. Derek was soaking his back in the hot tub when he looked at me and said, "You don't think Justin stole him, do you?"

I hadn't thought of it until that moment, but the wheels immediately started turning in my head. I said, "He wouldn't do that...would he?"

To this day, we don't know what happened to Catt Damon, but his disappearance and Justin's simultaneous departure seem like too great a coincidence not to be the reasonable explanation. And when Justin said he "wouldn't be able to volunteer regularly anymore," what he actually meant was he was never going to return, so...you do the math.

It was hard enough to think of Catt as being gone, but the thought of him being snagged by a predator in the woods or getting lost somewhere was a much worse scenario than the idea of his having been taken by somebody who loved him. I'd rather think he's safe and happy with Justin than any of the alternatives, so that's what I do.

The learning curve we had with Esther and managing our volunteers was huge, but it was nothing compared to what we needed to learn about running the sanctuary. Creating a sustainable sanctuary was the whole idea, and that included being absolutely certain we had all the insurance and legalities in place to protect us and the organizations we were creating. The "broken bone before brunch" incident also made us far more aware of what heavy tools we employed while working on the property, and who would be allowed to use them. For example, no handing chain saws to volunteers. Instead, we asked for people who owned their own tools to bring them along and to do specific jobs with them. We started being much more precise in giving directions, and we kept a close eye on the volunteers to make sure they didn't push themselves too hard.

It's easy to forget that many people don't do farm-type labor much these days. Hell, in this digital age, most of us don't do any type of manual labor much. We try to offer various jobs—some super easy, some more strenuous—and let people decide what they want to do. And every workday we learn something new, so we're constantly adjusting how we do things so as to keep everyone safe while still making their day fun and memorable. We want to start helping people expand upon the relationship they have with Esther through the Happily Ever Esther Farm Sanctuary and all of its residents.

Esther is just the key that opens the door. Happily Ever Esther Farm Sanctuary is what helps us drive our message home as people realize that every pig is like Esther. Every cow, every chicken, every single animal has just as much personality as a puppy. That's what we want everyone to know, and getting people to come back time and again is how we're going to achieve that.

CHAPTER TEN

By now, Esther was starting to show signs of her old personality from the Georgetown days: thankfully, she was calmer, friendlier, more relaxed. In retrospect, I guess I can see what happened. Teenage years already are tough on humans, right? And then when a teenager gets uprooted from home and has to acclimate to a new home, a new life? Everyone knows a lot of teens in that situation start acting out. And goodness knows Esther is about as humanlike as any animal you've ever met. She was going through a phase, I figure. It was no fun for her, and definitely no fun for us, but we survived it.

I was so happy to have my baby girl back, and it wasn't a moment too soon. I'd been ever more concerned that we had caused her so much trouble our first few months here that we'd never see the old Esther again. For a while, I thought I'd be forever rejected by her, treated the same way she treats the vet. It always made me laugh when Esther got strange with the vet. She wouldn't let him get near her, all because he had given her a needle one time. You know that old saying, "An elephant never forgets"? I swear it applies to pigs too. Their memories are incredible.

For example, when we lived in Georgetown, before the move, Esther once got into a box of Cheerios in the cupboard and took it into the living room. We managed to get most of them away from her, and then we sent her to the backyard so we could finish cleaning up. (Good luck ever trying to clean up after a 650-pound pig when she's still on-site.) She stayed out for well over an hour, having settled in for a yard nap after her customary rooting session in one of my once-incredible perennial gardens.

As soon as she came back inside, she went straight for the living room where we had confiscated the cereal, and proceeded to use her snout to lift the couch—so she could inspect underneath for lingering Cheerios. She didn't miss a beat. And that's how it always went: no matter how long it had been since something occurred, she remembered. It was the same with the vet. She associated him with a bad experience, and no matter what, she wasn't going to forget it.

Aside from the battles we would have in the forest, Esther rarely challenged us—or one of our house animals—for much of anything. Occasionally, we'd see a little scuffle over the bed, or who was going to finish the last kibble in the dog bowl. You know, the one that was sitting there all day until someone else expressed an interest in it, and now everyone wanted it.

But that peaceful, easy feeling lasted only a short while.

Yes, she was doing fine with her two dads (thank everything that is holy), but then she started showing some bold behaviors with the other animals. Previously, Shelby had been the "top dog." She ruled the roost as far as where she wanted to eat and sleep. If Shelby was lying in the middle of the room, Esther would walk completely around her, and Esther also gave Shelby plenty of space to eat at dinnertime. But as time passed at the farm, we started to see little glimmers of a rivalry between Esther and Shelby, mostly stemming from Esther.

Shelby's spot was in front of the sliding door. She loved to lie on the tiles once they'd been warmed up by the sun over the course of the day. It was probably much like a heating pad for her muscles, which at seventeen years old must have been getting a little stiff. But now, instead of just walking around Shelby or waiting for her to move, Esther would plow right through. Shelby wasn't used to this kind of behavior, so she would stand her ground with zero intention of moving. But that didn't matter to Esther. She was going where she wanted, whether Shelby moved or not. On more than one occasion, Esther stepped on Shelby's tail or knocked Shelby over as she barged on through. Esther was clearly starting to throw her weight around within our family herd structure. She was trying to move up in rank.

We didn't know this until we got to the farm, but family structure means everything to pigs in groups. The whole alpha concept is just as true for pigs as it is for dogs (and humans). There's always a top hog, and the others fall in line.

At some point, the top hog gets up there in age, and a younger one will challenge for top position. It's a common trait of pack animals, and it's not pretty to watch. It's no secret that Esther is a big girl, and when you have a 650-pound animal literally throwing her weight around, either you move or you get hurt. We understood that, but Shelby, who's all of seventy-five pounds soaking wet, wasn't catching the hint.

For months, we had been worried about losing our relationship with Esther due to her behavior, but we hadn't expected to also deal with a reshuffling of ranks within our group of four-legged family members. Derek and I had always assumed we were the bosses, but Esther had other plans, and they were adding yet another new dynamic to our family.

Around the same time, things were also starting to get a bit crazy in the barn. For the first time ever, we had to deal with multiple herds of pigs out there. Initially it was just Dan, Leonard, Bobbie, and Bear, and they got along beautifully. We had recently added April. She had gone into quarantine upon arrival, only to have her babies a few days later, well before we were able to do any integrating between April and the other pigs. The arrival of her piglets meant we would need to maintain the two herds indefinitely.

Dan and his piggy pals had been together for years, having arrived in unison from another sanctuary, but April didn't have a connection to Dan's group. Her mothering instincts were taking over, and she was ready to throw down anytime one of the other pigs came near her stall or walked up to the fences when her piglets were outside. We could tell the two herds weren't making friends with each other, and with the piglet situation, we decided we wouldn't even try to form one combined herd. They were two distinct family groups, and it looked like it would stay that way.

Space already was getting tight in there, and our experience with Esther told us it wasn't going to be very long before April and her crew outgrew their stall. We had just finished preparing space for B.J. and Escalade, along with making sure the other pigs had a secure pasture to explore. We now realized we would need even more space in the very near future. It hadn't even been a full year yet, and already we were approaching capacity for our barn.

Because the weather was warming up, we were able to move B.J. and Escalade from the barn into the pasture where the cows lived. That freed up a little space in the barn, which became the perfect place for our quickly expanding goat herd to live. With everybody's temporary living arrangements sorted out, we started planning our first "barn build."

Our cows had not yet come into the barn. Even when they had direct access, they seemed to prefer being outside. So we decided to build in the pasture behind the barn for our largest residents, moving the goats into B.J. and Escalade's old space. We looked online for design ideas and eventually decided on a twenty-four-by-sixteen-foot, board-and-batten building with a sheet-metal roof. We used six-by-six-inch posts, so if you literally drove a truck into the building, I suspect the truck would come out in worse condition than the building. It looks amazing, and the new addition finally allowed us to spread everyone out a little bit, taking advantage of some of the still-unused land we had available.

I know we hadn't been at the farm very long, at least in the big picture. But my mind moves a million miles a minute, and no matter how fast we worked, I always felt we could do more. We had barely scratched the surface of what was available to us and the animals, and sometimes it felt like such a battle to reclaim the neglected space. It was incredibly satisfying when we did it, and watching animals explore an area that had been "animal-free" for the better part of three decades was an amazing experience.

But as soon as we finished one space, I'd look past that field into the one beyond, noticing all the fallen trees and broken fences. It seemed like every moment of celebration was interrupted by the realization that we had barely even started on what we ultimately needed to do out there. Regardless, we knew to celebrate the small victories and not let ourselves get too overwhelmed with the upcoming workload.

As everyone got settled into their new living arrangements, we felt a huge weight lift from our shoulders. We have really thick skin, but when you put your life on social media, everybody becomes an expert on everything you do. We felt like we were constantly being judged for our actions: I don't know about you, but the daily caloric intake for a horse is a complete mystery to me. Or was, before we got a horse. We were always very aware of what we posted online, because we didn't want to get dragged into an argument with someone or have to defend ourselves. We had too much to do, and all of it was more important than dealing with internet trolls. But that's par for the course—it's something you accept when you open up your life to the world. And, ultimately, nothing was really happening that could have caused us a problem.

Until suddenly something did. Derek went out to the barn one afternoon and discovered what looked like a scene from a nineties slasher movie. There was blood all over the walls, on the doors, and in the straw.

Derek immediately called for me over his walkie-talkie, and just from how upset he sounded, I knew I needed to get there fast. I came running out of the house and into the barn, and I felt a wave of anxiety wash over me when I got my first glimpse of the scene.

Derek had already headed out the back door toward the forest. So without really getting a good look at what had happened or who was in there, I ran through the barn and out the back door, hopped the gate into the pigs' pasture, and followed Derek through the gate into the woods. That's where we found Leonard, lying on the ground with a gash in his leg that was about eight inches long and an inch deep.

My first thought: I had been working on fencing the day before and left a small section at the very end only partially secured. It was nailed to the post, but there were little wire ends a foot long that I still needed to wrap and secure. In the moment, I was sure Leonard had been caught by one of the wires, that this horrible injury was entirely my fault.

I was so upset, and even more so because I expected Derek was about to yell at me—until I saw Dan walk out of the barn in equally distressing condition. This hadn't been any fencing accident—it was a pig battle!

Leonard had unquestionably been the head of the pig herd, so much so that we never even considered that Dan might challenge him for top position. But Dan must have seen signs of weakness in Leonard and planned to capitalize on it, much as Esther was doing with Shelby.

Male pigs such as Dan and Leonard have massive tusks with tips as sharp as razor blades. The pigs use their heads like wrecking balls and will slam those tusks into an opponent as a defense mechanism. We don't know how this particular clash started, but it ended in a fight so serious that poor Leonard was too scared to even go back to the barn.

Dan clearly had come out on top of this particular melee, so we used kibble to lure him inside. Once we got him under control, we turned our attention to Leonard. We wanted to get him into the old barn where B.J. and Escalade lived before moving in with the cows. While there's never a good time for a pig fight, we were at least thankful this had happened when it had—and not a month earlier, when the barn was still totally full. After a bit, we secured Leonard and Dan in separate stalls while we waited for the vet to arrive.

Derek and I stayed in the barn, offering both our injured

fighters watermelon and grapes to keep their spirits up, but poor Leonard was having none of it. I've noted how expressive pigs are with their faces, particularly their eyes. Seeing Leonard after the fight was absolutely heartbreaking. He was usually so lively and enthusiastic, but now his head hung low, a look of total despair on his face. He had been defeated, and we didn't realize it at the time, but he'd never spend time with his lifelong friends again. His reign as king of the herd was over. He was devastated, and so were we. Until then, we'd seen such despair on the faces of pigs only when looking at photos of them in livestock trailers or at commercial farms.

The vet arrived and promptly confirmed that both pigs would require stitches. Leonard's wounds, he said, might even include muscle damage. The gash had gone clear through the skin and the heavy layer of fat pigs have, right into the leg muscles. That explained why Leonard was having such a hard time walking. His pain must have been excruciating. He couldn't stand up on that side, and as we knew from our experience with Esther, leg and foot injuries are not to be taken lightly with pigs. At Leonard's age and size, a bad leg could kill him.

The doctor immediately started stitching up the wounds. Dan went first because his were far less severe, and then it was Leonard's turn. During the procedure, the vet also suggested we trim both Leonard's and Dan's tusks to help prevent this from happening in the future. Removing pig tusks is a common practice in commercial settings—it's usually done when they're piglets, by brute force.

(Believe it or not, here's what a staff member at one of the animal hospitals said to us: "Know how we did that in my day? With a baseball bat." He accompanied this lovely comment with a gesture toward my face as if he were jamming the end of a bat into my mouth. It sent shivers up my spine and brought to mind how Esther must have lost her tail, most likely to a pair of pliers at the hand of some farm laborer.)

Luckily, female pigs don't have tusks anywhere near the size of those on males, so it's not quite the same issue with Esther. We didn't need to worry about trimming her tusks, because they simply weren't big enough to pose a serious problem. But Dan and Leonard are very well equipped to fight if need be, and we'd just witnessed firsthand how dangerous that could be.

Dr. Kirkham explained the process of trimming the tusks, reassuring us that it was 100 percent painless. However, he warned us, "they'll scream like jetliners." He continued: "You're not going to like it, it's not pretty, but I promise it won't hurt them." He explained the procedure thoughtfully, knowing we're extremely sensitive when it comes to our animals. He showed us the tool he was going to use. It was basically a long metal wire with small wooden handles on either end. It acts like a snare, looping over the pig's snout and top jaw and tightening. This causes the pig to freak out and try to escape by backing up. And this is where the "jetliner" thing comes in. The pig goes into complete panic mode, but once it hits the wall and has nowhere else to go, it just stands still with its mouth open, shrieking at an ear-piercing level. It honestly sounds like torture. Then the wire is used as a saw to cut the tusk above the nerve, similar to trimming a fingernail. Once the tusks are cut, the snare comes off, and the pig stops screaming and wanders off like nothing ever happened.

So the tusk-cutting itself is very easy; it's the snaring part that sucks. And Dr. Kirkham was right: we didn't like it one bit. After all the stories I've told about panicking anytime any of my animals dealt with any sort of trauma, did you think there was any chance I could shake this off? I might be getting a little better about handling these things, purely out of necessity, but let's face facts: all of my animals are family to me (and to Derek as well), and we can't stand seeing any of our children in pain or fear.

Unfortunately, this had to be done, at least in Dan's case. We knew there wasn't any other choice—if Dan and Leonard clashed again, Dan might just end up killing him. So you do what you have to do.

The vet trimmed Dan's tusks first, and the procedure went pretty smoothly, all things considered. As for Leonard, even though we knew the process itself wasn't a big deal, we were also considering Leonard's injured leg. We didn't want to cause him any panic that might lead to his injuring himself even more, so we decided not to trim his tusks at that time.

The situation with the two pigs was bad enough that we knew we couldn't chance another fight, so we planned to keep Leonard with Bear and move Dan and Bobbie into their own space.

In determining the logistics of who would go where, we immediately got to work securing the next pasture over. The plan was to move the goats from the old barn to the cow pasture, move the cows to the new pasture, and put Dan and Bobbie in the old barn. That left April and her babies in the same spot, with Leonard and Bear in the same space they had previously shared with Dan and Bobbie. Did you follow all that? We were having just as hard a time wrapping our heads around all the shuffling, but there was no alternative. The pressure was on to prep the new pasture as quickly as possible so we could get everyone moved.

Our brand-new cow barn was now taken over by goats and sheep, so that left the cows without shelter again: yet another item to add to our growing to-do list. Had it been winter, we would have had serious problems on our hands. But it was spring, so we had a few months to get another barn built. We focused on sorting the fences.

Just a few days after the fight, the great migration began. We moved Leonard into Bear's stall and put Dan and Bobbie in the old barn, which had its own little pasture. The goats settled into their nice new barn, and the cows took full advantage of their massive new pasture, even though it was still missing its barn.

All this time, things had been getting more complicated with our volunteer Ruth. We'd tried to remain hopeful that we could work through her control issues, but things were getting out of hand. It's one thing to act questionably on your own time; it's a whole other ball game when it happens right on the farm.

Ruth started making her own rules—she really was taking over. During public days, she would carry on as if the sanctuary were hers, telling people where they could go and what they could do. It was becoming very troubling for us, because her judgment was questionable a few times when incidents involving the animals occurred.

Lord knows we had more than our fair share of fencing. We had kept the goats in a fenced-in forest pasture for weeks without difficulty. But pigs aren't goats, and when we let some pigs in, we learned they were way too strong for the fencing we had in there.

After the weekend when the pigs escaped, we left a note that Monday asking Ruth not to let the pigs out. But she decided to let them out anyway. When we got to the barn and saw the pigs weren't in their stall, we immediately knew what had happened. Derek yelled for Ruth and asked where the pigs were; as soon as she started speaking, he cut her off: "The fences are down."

Derek immediately ran out the back of the barn toward the pen. Before we even got there, we could see the fence was even more bent than usual, and the pigs were gone. The pigs had crossed the service road and gone down into the ravine. It was super rocky, very steep, and covered in dense bush. That's not ideal pig terrain, much less people-searching-for-pigs terrain.

Within a few minutes, we located a few of the piglets in the ravine and started directing them back up toward the barn. They were pretty easy to move—thankfully not at all like Esther when we had our forest fights. Just as we rounded the corner with three of the five piglets, we saw the other two coming down the path between the two pastures immediately beside our barn. They were heading straight for Esther, who had since woken up and decided to join us outside for breakfast.

Here's the issue with that: Esther had never met another pig before without a fence separating her from the other pig. We knew she didn't like other pigs, and all of a sudden there were way more pigs than people in attendance, with nothing to keep the pigs apart.

My heart was in my throat, expecting it to become a literal battle. Esther was dramatically bigger than the piglets—she could injure or even kill several of them in a matter of seconds. (Yes, she's a sweetheart in most instances, but all of that goes out the window when it's a pig-versus-pig situation. That's just the nature of pigs.)

Mercifully, Esther seemed as perplexed about the situation as everyone else was. She honked and spun around as the piglets came running from all directions, but they went right past her and into the barn.

Afterward, Derek went to have words with Ruth. Things escalated to a yelling match, and Derek told her she was no longer welcome at the farm. It was hard on everyone. We knew

Ruth had been trying to help, but we couldn't take chances when it came to the safety of our animals, and the piglet situation could have turned out so much worse. We were incredibly lucky that no one was hurt. Our experience with Ruth led to the creation of a volunteer-coordinator position, a thorough review of our policies surrounding who comes to the farm, and very specific guidelines covering what can and cannot be done. It was sad to lose Ruth, but it was a beneficial learning experience in moving forward with the sanctuary.

We had to focus on dealing with the pig situation. We had figured for a while that we would need to create another pig herd at some point, but we always assumed that would consist of splitting up April and her piglets once the babies got a little older. Susie Coston at Farm Sanctuary had warned us that fights among pigs were almost guaranteed, but we'd figured that would consist of the piglets eventually trying to establish their roles in the herd. But then Dan and Leonard surprised us with their fight. It was yet another huge learning experience for us. With them split up, we now had three pig herds, plus the potential of another looming battle among April's offspring. There was no time to relax; we needed to prepare for a fourth herd. This looked like it would be a never-ending cycle.

We figure we'll just need to keep building as we bring in more animals.

CHAPTER ELEVEN

B y the time fall came around, we were exhausted. We'd
been going full-tilt in nonstop activity for what seemed
like a lifetime. In reality, it had been only two years since
all this madness began, and things had been happening so
quickly we hadn't had an opportunity to process it all, never
mind take time off to reflect.

Derek had been able to get away to visit his parents in
Northern Ontario a couple of times, and I had gone to a few
Highland games here and there. But we hadn't taken time
off together since well before Esther the Wonder Pig had
become a sensation online. The coming winter was going to
be our downtime. We didn't have plans to leave the farm,
but, for once, there would be no crowdfunding campaigns,
no workdays, no fences to build. Okay, technically, there
were lots of fences to build, but winter makes working outside all but impossible for most tasks, so no fences would be
built until spring.

We finally saw a window with a little bit of time for us to

take a breather. We even had a new woodstove and wood to burn, so we knew our heating issues—although not over, because hauling wood is no picnic—were squared away for a while. And hauling wood still beats a $1,200 monthly electric bill for so little heating that it still leaves you, your pig, and your pipes frozen.

Compared to the previous two years, being basically alone on the farm for a couple of months sounded like an ideal holiday. But then I got an invitation from a foundation based in Exuma, in the Bahamas, to visit the world-famous swimming pigs—the latest viral travel trend. You travel to an otherwise-deserted tropical island full of wild pigs that come swimming out to greet visitors arriving on boats.

To us, obviously, this sounded like paradise. When we checked it out online, the pictures provided very much the same impression. We'd heard about this place for years. Every week, Esther's fans sent us numerous articles and photos with accompanying messages such as "Have you seen this?" or "Esther needs to go swimming in the Bahamas." But there was also the occasional "I don't like the looks of this; something's not right."

Put a pin in that: you can bet we'll be coming back around to it later.

The island had become one of those places we put on our bucket list, knowing full well people who run animal sanctuaries don't really get to take holidays. But this wasn't exactly an invitation, according to the organizers who contacted us; they said they wanted our opinion on how they could improve things.

They assured us the pigs were really well cared for, fed, and watered daily, and that their lives were as grand as could be. They also promised us the pigs were never used for food, that the locals all loved them, and they'd been there for years.

The story most commonly told to tourists is that these pigs were brought to the islands back in the pirate days. They'd get dropped off while the pirates went off and did their pirate thing, returning to harvest a pig for food as required. It makes sense, but it's been awhile since Blackbeard sailed the sea, so I didn't really put too much stock in the legend.

Regardless, I shared the info with Derek, who had been dying to take a tropical vacation since the last time I dragged him around Europe for three weeks. He loves to travel as much as I do, but he's much more of a peace-and-quiet kind of guy. Derek travels to kick back and rest in breathtaking environments, not to take your destination by storm—which (no surprise to anyone) is what I prefer.

During our European trip, I had us scheduled to be in a different city pretty much every other day. We picked up a rental car in Amsterdam and then ripped through Germany, Switzerland, France, Belgium, and back to the Netherlands over the course of a week and a half. We drank beer from a boot in Germany, jumped three hundred feet into a canyon in Switzerland, and explored the Palace of Versailles in

France. It was a dream vacation for me, but Derek's dream vacation involves palm trees and a wristband that entitles him to bottomless piña coladas all week.

Exuma was our chance for him to enjoy just such a tropical paradise, and bonus: it also happened to have pigs we could swim with. The offer was for a five-day, four-night trip in the Bahamas. The organizers would cover our accommodations, get us to the pigs, and show us around—all we had to provide was our own transportation to the island. It seemed easy enough, and I let the excitement of the idea get to me before Derek brought up the fact that we now had a farm that needed to be minded if we wanted to go anywhere.

Huh. Good point. Dammit.

Where was I going to find someone who could care for our house and our 650-pound daughter and manage the sanctuary?

It was no small ask, but one person immediately came to mind.

Her name was Kim, and we had met her, like so many others, via Esther's Facebook page. She actually responded to one of my tweets asking for a referral to a creative bakery that would craft a fun cake for Esther's second birthday. Kim didn't know a bakery, but she sent pictures of a carved watermelon pig and offered to make it for us. We'd been in touch ever since, and Kim had more recently been coming to the farm frequently.

We knew Kim was familiar with how things went in the

barn, Esther was good with her, and Kim had been telling us to take a few days off for months. She offered her help all the time, but we weren't yet comfortable enough to leave. However, this Exuma trip was not only intriguing because it was in the Caribbean, but it also was only four nights... a trial trip, really. It wasn't one of the marathon three-week vacations we had taken before. We'd really only be gone for little more than a long weekend. Kim happily agreed to step in for us while we traveled, and I excitedly confirmed our plans with the folks in Exuma.

I recalled the skeptical notes about the island we'd gotten from some of our fans, but in today's world, it's normal to have virtually everything—no matter how objectively wonderful—attract some critics. We hadn't seen anything online that caused great concern, and I greatly hoped the same would be true when we got there.

We were scheduled to visit the island in mid-January. I hadn't used travel points in ages for anything, and since we'd moved, I'd spent a small fortune on my credit card. So I splurged and used my points to book us business-class seats. We had everything organized and were confident we had covered all our bases. But you know how it goes: you don't realize you forgot something until it's too late.

We had forgotten to consider one crucial detail: Shark Week. And I'm not talking about the Discovery Channel's annual weeklong event.

Two days before we were scheduled to leave, the telltale

signs of Esther's monthly "lady days" became apparent. She gets restless, goes outside at all hours of the night to patrol our fences, and challenges anyone who gets in her way. Forgetting this was a major oversight, and it nearly derailed our entire trip. We were super excited to get away, but we both also had a nagging sense of anxiety over the countless things that could go wrong. We generally had never left Esther for more than a day or two since she was a piglet, and one time when we did leave her for three days, we came home to a virtual swimming pool–volume of urine in our basement. Now we were facing the same situation again, but this time our one-time piglet was 650 pounds!

We explained the situation to Kim, but she had seen Esther during Shark Week before and kept telling us not to worry.

"I've got it," she'd say. "No problem. You're going away, so stop it!"

One consideration that made this different from the old days in Georgetown: if shit hit the fan, the barn was always available. Of course, Esther had never spent a single night in the barn, but at least we knew it was an option Kim could employ should our daughter become unmanageable. It wasn't an ideal scenario, but if push came to shove, it would work. Derek and I both realized we really needed the break, and who knew how long it would be before an opportunity like this one would present itself again. So we stuck to our plans: we were going to the beach come hell or high water.

When departure day arrived, we bounced out of bed for our 6 a.m. flight, quickly reviewed the procedures with Kim for the fifth (okay—let's be honest—tenth) time, and then kissed everyone goodbye and headed to the airport. The flight was terrific (gotta love business class), and as we made our approach, the scenery was incredible. I had never been to the Caribbean before; the water around the Bahamas was just extraordinary. We were both so excited to get to the hotel and kick back with a cocktail.

We arrived early Sunday and weren't going to see the pigs until Tuesday, so we would have almost two days to just do nothing. (Heaven!) We were met at the airport by Paula, a representative from the foundation, and she took us to the island. She was from Montreal but spent a lot of time in Exuma, so she was exceptionally familiar with what was happening there. She showed us around on our way to the resort—about a thirty-minute drive from the airport—and pulled into a gas station about twenty minutes into the drive.

"I figured you guys would want to grab a few things right away," Paula said. "It's a holiday tomorrow, so everything will be closed."

I didn't think anything of this and really didn't fully grasp what she'd said. Honestly, I assumed it was a souvenir store, or something to that effect, because she knew we wouldn't have a ton of time to explore the island otherwise.

"We're good," I said. "All I need is my wristband and a piña colada."

She laughed with me, but under her breath, she added: "I wish."

"Are you not staying at the same resort as us?" I asked. She was there so much, I thought maybe she stayed at an off-site condo or something.

"Oh yeah," she said. "Of course I'm staying there...but there are no wristbands involved. You've gotta buy your own cocktails."

My heart sank immediately.

I had told Derek we were heading to the "Villas at Sandals Emerald Bay," an all-inclusive resort. But there had clearly been a miscommunication. Paula explained that we were staying at the "Villas at Emerald Bay," a self-catering villa complex right by Sandals, but not in any way associated with that resort.

The friggin' bay is literally called Emerald Bay, with two distinct resorts: the Villas and the Sandals. Ugh.

I went from cloud nine to being ready to cry in a fraction of a second. As Paula explained the misunderstanding, I could see Derek getting upset in the backseat. Eventually he just got out of the car and walked into the store without saying anything. I excused myself and followed him in.

He whirled on me as soon as I walked in. "How did this happen?"

"I have no idea," I said. It was all I could say, knowing full well my excitement about the potential holiday was totally to blame. I didn't bother to ask the right questions. I made assumptions, and every single one of them was biting us in the ass.

When I initially Googled "Emerald Bay Exuma," all that came up was the Sandals resort, with a link on its page for the beachfront villas on the property. (They looked spectacular, by the way.) I didn't go any further. The organizers had told me we'd be at the Villas at Emerald Bay, and I just assumed that was part of the Sandals resort.

Derek and I had traveled almost two thousand miles to a Caribbean island under the impression that everything was taken care of for us. We hadn't budgeted $1.50 for a single apple from the grocery store, much less $15 for a piña colada from the hotel bar.

So it's safe to say our visit had gotten off to a rough start. But the situation improved quickly. When we arrived at the villa complex, we discovered it was absolutely stunning. It was built by some big hoity-toity hotel brand and then sold as private units. Gorgeous!

Our villa was basically a house: two stories, with marble floors and rich mahogany trim on the doors and the ceiling. It had a master bedroom and a guest bedroom on the main floor. The master had a giant en suite bathroom with granite counters and a huge glass "party shower." Both bedrooms had exit doors that opened onto covered patios overlooking the garden. Upstairs was another bathroom and a full living room, dining room, and kitchen—all finished in a Bahamian style. The ceilings were vaulted, and they anchored large ceiling fans shaped like palm leaves. The balcony opened off the dining room, letting us look out on multimillion-dollar yachts in the marina across from a golf cart path that wound its way through the complex and its golf course.

Around the corner, literally a one-minute walk away, were the pool and the restaurant/bar. Thatched roofs covered a tiled bar and seating area, while little waterfalls splashed into the infinity pool with the ocean beyond. It was the kind of place that looked like it belonged in a magazine.

Derek and I were totally out of our element. Everyone loves nice things, but nice usually means very expensive. We sat down for dinner and saw one item on the menu we could eat, a chickpea curry dish served over rice. It was delicious. Derek even convinced me to order my first island piña colada in God knows how many years. We sat out by the pool for most of the evening, taking in the view, slowly drinking our ridiculously expensive drinks until close to midnight. It was all quite lovely, but the bill for both of us was close to $100, and that was just for one meal. We knew we'd need to rein it in for the next few days, because spending $100 three times a day for four days was not an option for us.

Having disposable income was a thing of the past since leaving our careers and trying to establish the sanctuary. We couldn't afford to spend that kind of money, so we spent most of the first two days in the villa, eating pasta and tomato sauce we had picked up at the corner store on our way in. Derek would go down to the beach to read or lie in the sun with a drink for a few hours. But in my mind, things weren't going to plan, so I sulked in the room watching TV, wishing I were home. I tried to keep my mind on the light at the end of the tunnel: the swimming pigs. It had been on my bucket list since I learned of this magical tropical paradise known as Pig Beach.

Paula arranged to meet us bright and early on Tuesday morning and would be escorting us for the day. Pig Beach was about a thirty-minute drive from the villa complex along mostly narrow, dirt roads. Exuma is a fairly flat island, and it must get hit pretty hard by tropical storms, because the vegetation seemed limited to mangroves and other small-to-medium shrubs once we left the immaculately manicured property surrounding the villa.

We talked the entire drive about everything from the swimming pigs to our lives before Esther. We'd gotten to know Paula pretty well, having sat with her after dinner for a few hours the night we arrived. She grew up in Saudi Arabia and worked in the airline industry before meeting her husband. I love planes, and I want to get my pilot's license one day, so as soon as she brought up the airline industry we had plenty to talk about.

She also gave us the lowdown on why they'd wanted us to come down in the first place. They knew there were some concerns about the welfare of the pigs, and their growing popularity meant it was only a matter of time before somebody tried to shine a less-flattering light on what was going on there. She told us about the man who cared for the pigs, how he went out every day with water and food. She also explained that a few copycat locations close by had capitalized on the concept of swimming pigs, and now multiple tiny islands had herds of pigs on them. We asked again if the pigs were being eaten and got a resounding, "Oh God no, these pigs are safe."

Overall, the general tone was very positive, and we were going in there with lots of ideas for things they could do to make sure it was actually "Paradise for Pigs." We saw a huge opportunity for them to educate people: a sanctuary in a tropical setting, where pigs are free to do whatever they want. It sounded almost too good to be true.

When we arrived at the beach, we met the man who cared for what they called the Original Swimming Pigs. We boarded his boat with about ten other people who were just there for the tour. It was going to be about half a day, with stops at the highest point in Exuma, a beach full of wild ocean iguanas and, of course, the famous swimming pigs.

Our very first stop was to see the pigs, about forty-five minutes into the tour. As the boat came around the corner, I could see Pig Beach straight ahead, recognizing the surroundings from photos on the social media page. "Oh my God, this is it!" I said to Derek, scrambling to get my phone ready so I could take a video of the pigs' coming out to meet us.

As soon as the pigs noticed the boat, they scurried out of the bushes and onto the sand, some even coming straight into the water, waiting for us to get within range. When we got about a hundred feet out, they started swimming. I nearly died. Little black-and-white pigs, each about 250 to 300 pounds, swimming directly toward us.

It was magical. Everyone on board lit up with excitement. There's not a whole lot going on in Exuma, so for many, this was why they'd come. While the rest of the passengers rushed to take their photos, a crewmate started gathering supplies to take ashore, including food and a few barrels of fresh water. He also had a cooler of snacks for us to hand-feed the pigs, and he started handing them out to everyone on board. I happily turned around to accept mine, and that's when my excitement turned to horror.

I had been given a hot dog to feed the pigs.

Seriously?

My heart was in my throat. Trying to keep it together, I turned to show Derek, who didn't do quite as good a job of containing his revulsion. "You've got to be kidding me," he said with a look of disgust.

Then Derek turned to the crewmate: "Are these pork dogs? You better not be feeding pork to these pigs." He said this very loudly, so everyone could hear.

"No, they're chicken dogs," the man replied.

Paula saw the whole scene unfolding and jumped in quickly to prevent what was clearly just seconds from turning into a huge donnybrook.

"These are the kinds of things we want to talk about with

you guys," she said. "Put the hot dogs down, and let's just go to the beach and meet the pigs."

Derek was beside himself as he climbed down the ladder and walked ashore. He kept to himself for about twenty minutes, walking around to take in Pig Beach. I walked with Paula and spoke to her about what we were seeing.

It wasn't pretty.

The beach was littered with trash and consisted mostly of jagged coral rocks, because the sand had been washed away by a recent storm. The highest point on the little island appeared to be only about fifteen feet high—nothing a solid wave couldn't crash over—with little more than mangled thorny bushes to provide cover from the sun.

We saw close to thirty pigs that day, some as big as Esther, with matching cropped tails to boot. Remember that legend about the pirates? It should be amended to note that the pirates were really just "some guy who shipped over a few pigs from Miami." Now, I cannot say with absolute certainty that at some point pirates didn't bring pigs to these islands, but the pigs there now sure as hell aren't descendants of them.

The island was tiny and rampant with piglets that far outnumbered the larger pigs. The claim that no one ate the pigs suddenly seemed questionable as well. The population was totally uncontrolled; if left unchecked, it would be out of hand in no time. Someone was making sure that the pig population didn't get too big, and it wasn't via selective sterilization of baby pigs to prevent breeding.

There also were no permanent shelters anywhere; the closest approximation was a small wood-frame box the smallest piglets could climb into to escape the larger pigs. The only place the larger pigs could go to get out of the relentless sun was under the thornbushes, but even those offered only dappled shade at best.

We saw a number of the larger pigs, some pink-skinned like Esther, covered in moles and black spots that looked like potential skin cancer. Pigs are prone to sunburn just like humans. Can you imagine spending years in the sun without sunscreen, how painful that would be? It was as if someone pulled up with a boat, tossed out a bunch of pigs, and left them alone to figure out life.

The resorts make thousands of dollars from people coming to see the pigs, and apparently they do donate some food. But the food we saw getting dropped off at the beach had Derek picking ham bones out of it. No big deal.

It was clear to us that no one ever took the time to ensure the pigs were eating safe, proper food. We found that devastating, and it only got worse when we asked about their medical care. We were told they had never been visited by a vet. There isn't even a permanent vet on Exuma—at least there wasn't when we went—never mind a vet to take care of those poor pigs. Everything about Pig Beach was the opposite of what we had thought it would be. The pigs were still beautiful and full of personality, but they weren't living in paradise by any stretch of the imagination.

It became obvious that the man who cared for the pigs was now aware of who we were. I don't think Paula had been totally up front with him about the fact that she was bringing in two vegan animal advocates to see his operation. He was clearly frustrated. I'm sure he assumed we were going to be troublemakers, but that's the last thing we wanted to be. We knew if we kicked up a fuss, it would be the pigs that would suffer. Rather than pointing fingers and blasting the guy—much as we desperately wanted to do exactly that—we knew we had to take a diplomatic approach. (Yes, believe it or not, I'm capable of that on occasion.)

Our mind-set: From all the brochures of this place, you'd expect to see pigs in paradise, and while that was partially true—the pigs did live on a beach in the Bahamas—it was so far from paradise. Their living conditions were atrocious. The inbreeding was rampant. They had fresh water only while people were visiting on the island; the rest of the time, they were fresh out of luck. The poor pigs were out there being burned to a crisp every day. The business owners said they had shelter and a controlled area for the piglets, but they didn't. The shelter was prickly bushes that provided almost no shade, and the controlled area for the piglets was a few pieces of wood with gaps too small for the large pigs to get into. The small piglets could go in, which was okay, but nobody else could.

We had been at Pig Beach for close to an hour when the captain said it was time to leave for our next stop. I went to get Derek, who was gathering garbage on the beach to distract himself from the scene around us. He had tears in his eyes as we got on the boat to pull away. I think we both felt as if we were letting the pigs down; we had inadvertently become supporters of something we knew was wrong. Paula spoke to the captain during the ride to our next stop, and the captain came over to me as they tied off the boat so everyone could go ashore. There was nothing at this spot. It was a tiny island with a big hill, the highest point in Exuma, and cliffs dropping off into the ocean on the other side. It was just a beautiful photo opportunity.

I strolled around with the captain, expressing our concerns. I could tell he was worried about what we had to say, but deep down there was also a hint of genuine concern. I could tell he loved those pigs, and in that moment, I actually started to feel bad for him. I now knew firsthand how expensive food was down there. Nobody can afford to spend $1.50 on an apple, especially if you're buying 250 to 300 apples a week. And that's just piggy snack food, never mind getting your hands on nutritionally balanced pig meals. It costs us about $10 for a twenty-five-kilogram bag of pig food. In Exuma, it would be quadruple that.

The captain told me about issues with the local government, about getting permission to build appropriate shelters. It was starting to seem like he was doing the best he could, but that he had very little support from local officials. The resorts were bringing in huge amounts of money as a direct result of these pigs, but it was too much work for them to ensure donated food got separated so the pigs wouldn't be eating pigs? And the Bahamas Ministry of Tourism had posters all over the islands, in magazines, and online, but it couldn't assist with the construction of shelters, or even help persuade other governing agencies to grant permission to the pigs' caretakers to build them? And what about the Humane Society? Where was it in all of this? And why was it that these pigs, who brought money into the islands hand over fist, couldn't even get an appointment with a veterinarian?

These agencies were all super happy to advertise and promote their Pig Beach tourist attraction, and had no issue taking the money the pigs brought in, but they didn't ask anyone to take some of that money and use it to properly care for the pigs. There was also the issue with copycat pig islands popping up. None of these groups spoke to each other. So it was a total free-for-all, and none of them would help any of the others.

While I was expressing my frustration to Paula later that day, she referred to the concept of Black Crab Syndrome—you might have heard it just called crab mentality. When two or more crabs get trapped in a hole, they drag down other crabs around them in an effort to save themselves, instead of helping each other. Because they're incapable of cooperating, they all end up dead in the hole. Paula said that was basically what happened in the Bahamas, specifically among the various islands with pigs. They were all competing, and it was like the Wild West with no one enforcing any welfare rules or safety precautions.

Thinking about the pigs consumed the rest of our day. Derek and I wound up sitting on the patio at the restaurant in the villa complex late into the night with Paula. We expressed our concerns and brainstormed ways we could help.

We discussed arranging a visit from our vet and his team. We thought perhaps we could get them down to the island to neuter all the males, which would immediately deal with overpopulation concerns. They could do a health check on every pig and address any urgent medical issues. They also could provide the caretakers with a basic understanding of pig health and show them how to administer medical treatment for abrasions, questionable moles and lumps, and the various injuries that can occur no matter how well you care for your pigs. From there, we could work to get the relevant government agencies involved regarding construction of suitable weatherproof shelters. We could hold the Humane Society accountable for providing the required ongoing and emergency medical support currently unavailable to the pigs.

We also needed to stop the lies about pirates having left the pigs on the islands in days gone by. They may have been historically accurate, but none of the current pigs had anything to do with the pirate pigs. They were put there for the sole purpose of telling a legend. The true story was that some of the pigs were, allegedly, rescued from commercial operations in Miami. Fine. So say so. Tell tourists so they know that these beautiful swimming pigs were bred to be dinner but were rescued.

Considering the number of people who visit the beach, the opportunity to educate them in meaningful ways was astonishing, but it got completely lost in folklore and misinformation. Instead of taking advantage of everyone's enthusiasm for these pigs to provide information about their intelligence or social structure, they hand you a hot dog and tell you to pick up only the little pigs because the big ones might bite. I mean, really?

We flew home a couple of days later, disappointed but enthusiastic about the possibilities to help make things better.

Everything at home was fine. Well, "fine." Kim was miserable, but the house was intact. Esther apparently wanted to go outside every ninety minutes, and Kim got no sleep and also couldn't get the fire going. We have no idea how she survived, but she did. And she even agreed to watch Esther on our next vacation.

Just a few weeks after we arrived home, a news report appeared about the swimming pigs and the situation that was unfolding down there. Someone else with knowledge of pig care had seen exactly what we had, and that person wrote about it!

The article was brought to our attention immediately, because people knew we had just been there, and everyone wanted our opinion. They forced our hand. Our plan had been to get some pieces in place to help out down there, and then tell everyone not only what we had seen but what was being done to fix it. The article changed all that, because now we had no choice but to validate its contents. We couldn't disagree with a word of the article. But we tried to follow our confirmation of the islands' problems with the numerous ways they could be fixed, how there was indeed potential for the proper tropical pig sanctuary that we all envisioned when we saw the pictures of Pig Beach online. That's the one thing the article was missing. Yes, there were problems, but had anyone done anything to try to fix them? Was anyone helping to address these concerns, or had they been ongoing and ignored for years? At some point, you absolutely need to call somebody out for doing wrong. But there's also a time to work with the person on fixing the problems from the inside in a way that creates lasting and meaningful change.

Educating people is the only way to create change, and that's pretty much impossible when the person in question is on the defensive. That's exactly what happened when word of the article got back to the guy who took care of the pigs we saw. He became extremely angry and immediately blamed us, no matter how much we reassured him that we had nothing to do with it. All lines of communication were severed.

From the minute we saw those pigs, we worried that stomping our feet about the situation would only hurt them. They were our top priority. We wanted to help, but it was becoming increasingly clear that just wasn't going to happen. Black Crab Syndrome struck again. To the best of my knowledge, to this day those pigs have no shelter, no reliable source of fresh water, no healthy pig food, and no access to medical care. But the people who make their living off them, of course, are doing just fine.

I truly hope that one day Pig Beach will become the paradise it could be, but I can tell you without a shadow of a doubt that we'll never go back. The people in charge need to do the right thing for the pigs, not just for their pocketbooks. If they don't, the beach needs to be shut down.

Our first "vacation" in years was a bust. Not that it wasn't an incredible spot, but we just couldn't stop thinking about the pigs. Whenever you book a vacation, you're inundated with options for excursions or day trips, and many of those feature encounters with animals. We had never given much thought to it before, even after adopting Esther and starting the sanctuary.

Granted, we would never go to a place like SeaWorld. But the swimming pigs seemed different, much like open-water swimming with dolphins. It feels like the dolphins are wild, and like you're in this magical place. Well, at least that's true until the trainer blows his whistle and the dolphins return to their pen by the shore. You realize they're no more free than the dolphins at SeaWorld. But we buy into the illusion that they are because it makes us feel better about participating. The resort presents us with a story that makes it all sound so fantastic, because if it told us the truth, no one would ever go.

A few weeks after we got home from Exuma, we got a call from my dad, who's a travel agent based in Scotland. He had been on a trip of his own, attending a convention, where he got to chatting with Marilisa, a rep from Carnival Cruise Line. It turned out she knew about Esther and was a follower, so she and my dad quickly hit it off. Before long, they were discussing the idea of hosting an Esther Cruise to raise money for the sanctuary. My father was extremely excited about this potential cruise, but we weren't really feeling it at first. It was a huge undertaking, and to be honest, I didn't think anyone would want to go.

Regardless, I agreed to take a meeting with Marilisa, so she visited Derek and me at the farm. We spoke for a few hours about all the things we were worried about: food, fund-raising potential, bringing in guest speakers, and hosting special events. The more we talked about it, the more our heads started to spin with all the details being thrown our way. Still, we loved that it was unique, and the potential to get Esther's message in front of a whole new audience was incredible. So we took another leap of faith and secured 250 cabins.

We were told we'd be able to hold those cabins with no risk to us for a certain amount of time, and then release any unsold cabins back to Carnival. The financial risk was very limited, but the time commitment and organization required was another story. We knew we couldn't sell an entire ship, but we thought if we could get a few hundred people on board by ourselves, we potentially would have a much larger captive audience to expose to our lifestyle. Think about it: around two thousand people literally trapped on the ocean, surrounded by vegans. What could possibly go wrong?

The potential drama aside, we viewed it as a huge opportunity to show those people how fun we (vegans) are and how amazing the food can be. We could promote conversation with people who might never have heard of Esther, and we could correct their misconceptions about what it actually means to be a vegan.

There's always a method to our madness. The cruise wasn't just about making money for the farm; it was about broadcasting our message to a whole new audience. We also saw opportunities with Carnival. We were having meetings and phone calls with reps at the head office, so we had our foot in the door. If we played our cards right, we'd have the opportunity to build relationships and ultimately ask for a meeting with someone higher up the chain. On our particular cruise, Carnival was going to expand its "Esther-Approved" offerings. If we could get other cruisers to take advantage of these options, perhaps we could get Carnival to make lasting changes on its menus moving forward.

Carnival is the largest cruise company in the world, and getting its executives to take a meeting at some point was (and is) a very important aspect of our master plan. We weren't going to demand that anyone change anything—we were just going to show them why increasing vegan options was the most logical, sensible decision they could make.

Things came together pretty quickly. In addition to the "Esther-Approved" menu for our guests, they'd make available a special "Esther Cocktail" at the bars, and even stock their pizza bar with dairy-free cheese. We arranged to bring along guest speakers and even planned a beach party on one of the islands. It would feature little piggy floaties and coolers full of beer, followed by a pub crawl on the ship later that night.

It was all coming together, but something was missing: animals. Esther couldn't be with us, but how could we incorporate animals into our trip in a way that was consistent with our overall message? Then it hit us: Why weren't we looking for a sanctuary to visit? That would be perfect, but what were the chances of finding a proper animal sanctuary on a Caribbean island? Not very good, we figured. But after a little research, we were happily proven wrong.

We found a donkey sanctuary in Aruba, which happened to be one of the islands the cruise was going to visit. We contacted the managers to see if they would be open to having our group come for a workday instead of just a tour, so we could actually help out. We didn't just want to go scratch a bunch of asses; we wanted to do something meaningful.

With the sanctuary on board, we had nailed down our

itinerary and were ready for the First Annual Esther Cruise. The reaction was amazing. We managed to sell almost all of our cabins by the time we sailed. From the time we decided to try the cruise idea until we actually set sail, about one year passed. So we had plenty of time to work out all the details to make it extra special for our guests.

We made Esther cruise shirts, brought along plenty of giveaways like jewelry and books, and brought a bunch of little inflatable pigs that we would leave lying around the ship. By the end of the week, there were sixty of them floating around—you could see some sitting in windows when we got off at our last port of call. It had literally become the Esther Cruise. We had taken over the ship. Everyone on board wanted to know, "What's the deal with the pig group?"

We had people joining our events and chatting up members of the group left, right, and center. People naturally want to be part of the fun crowd. Our group brought a party with them everywhere we went, and it was infectious. We had an absolute blast, and aside from the odd minor mix-up, the trip went off without a hitch.

It's hard to say what was the best part, but I think many would agree that our visit to the donkey sanctuary was the highlight. We spent the day cleaning up, painting a storage shed, and meeting all the animal residents. The sanctuary now has a mural we all had a hand in painting. If you look closely, you'll find Esther on it.

We left our mark in Aruba in a really beautiful way. We

were able to donate a few thousand dollars to the sanctuary, thanks in part to a suggested $20 donation we requested from each guest, but also thanks to the amazing bus company that drove us from the ship to the sanctuary. We explained why we were going, and they were so incredibly supportive, they offered to stop on the way so we could get fresh fruit and veggies for the donkeys. They even reduced the rental rate so we could donate our savings to the donkeys. A few guests actually "adopted" donkeys, in a financial-support sense, so they could support the facility post-visit. The cruise turned out so wonderfully that we immediately started planning the second one. We hope to make it an annual event and to make it bigger and better every year. Who knows, maybe one day we will take over an entire ship, and we'll get to help a whole lot of animals by doing it.

EPILOGUE

By the time you read this, we'll be approaching our fourth anniversary at the farm. It feels like a lifetime. That's in part because of the pace at which we've been moving since a so-called mini-pig came into our lives, and partially because of how drastically our lives have changed in what ultimately has been a very short amount of time.

And it was all due to Esther.

Since Derek and I got together almost eighteen years ago and before Esther came along, we had been working our asses off to build our version of the perfect life. We hadn't achieved it yet, but we had the vision and were on our way. We had our house, our fur family, great jobs, and the freedom to do what we pleased. We had fallen into a very comfortable routine, and if not for Esther, we probably never would have changed it.

The world is huge, and it's often scary, so it's easy to sit back and just keep doing what you do. It can take something drastic to give you that initial push, to force you to take that first step. For us it was a smiling pig named Esther. Getting to know her ignited a fire from embers I'd like to think we always had inside us but just hadn't yet been sparked.

The first step for us was going vegan and realizing that didn't necessarily mean we needed to pick up signs and start marching in the streets. As someone who hadn't thought burgers were burgers without bacon, I was making a departure of monumental proportions from my earlier lifestyle. I didn't think I could do it, but seeing Esther's face every morning was a reminder that it wasn't just about me. There's more to life than what makes me happy. Especially when that happiness comes at the expense of animals like Esther.

There I was, doing something I would have told you was impossible just a few years earlier. If Esther hadn't come along, we never would have realized the potential we had to make a meaningful impact on the world. You know how it goes. But we found ourselves stepping outside of our little bubble when we started the Esther the Wonder Pig Facebook page.

For the first time in our lives, we were on the receiving end of messages about how we had impacted someone else's life. Two men from a little town in Southern Ontario were influencing the lives of people on the other side of the world. Realizing that you have the ability to do something you never thought you could is unbelievably empowering in its own right. Finding out you can help someone else do the same thing just takes it to a whole new level! This was what allowed us to follow a path that seemed impassable, even to the people who knew us best. Leaving behind everything we thought we wanted? Starting a brand-new life we knew nothing about—specifically, running a sanctuary? Some friends laughed at us, and some left us, but much to our surprise, the majority stayed with us. They became the most amazing cheerleaders as we set off on this new adventure.

Such rapid change is still scary, but it's also exhilarating. We've learned new things, met new people, and found a confidence in ourselves we thought was reserved for those corny motivational posters in office buildings everywhere. (If you can't grasp the concepts of teamwork or achievement without a poster, we're amazed you managed to dress yourself and arrive at the office in the first place.)

What's the secret? Was it magic piggy powers? Or did we just set a goal and get to work trying to achieve it? Our actions were inspired, certainly, but we had to make them happen on our own, inspired or not. There was no special potion; we just followed our gut instinct, even when most other people thought we'd fail.

As Esther's pages continue to grow in popularity, so too does the number of ways she is making her mark on the lives of people she connects with. We have made a conscious effort to maintain an upbeat, funny tone on our pages. We've refined the way we present our message to make sure it remains positive and engaging. We focus on building relationships with people, but those relationships are not with us—they're with Esther. We do our best to empower her fans with information and stories that help them understand why we do what we do. But we're extremely careful to do that in a way that's not off-putting or preachy. We've found that to be the most engaging way of promoting a vegan lifestyle to a broad spectrum of people.

We had a lady from the southern United States write us with thanks for teaching her young sons that it's okay to have two dads. It let them see that families might look different, but fundamentally we're all the same. That's the sort of lesson we never intended to communicate through Esther—it's just a fortunate by-product, but we're thrilled it worked out that way.

We also had a lady from Ottawa, Ontario, let us know that not only had Esther's photos become her "happy place" when she was having a bad day, but they also had become a means to communicate with her mother, who was suffering from dementia. One day, the lady was sitting beside her mom's hospital bed, watching a video on our Facebook page, and she decided to show her mother the screen. They both sat there smiling at a video of Esther doing her thing—opening the fridge and harassing Derek for a bite of whatever he was eating. This supporter said it was the first time in months she had seen her mom smile, and it meant the world to her.

Who knew a pig could mean so much to so many people? Esther has an uncanny ability to make people happy, forget about everything else for a few minutes, and just have a laugh.

That has been our goal from the minute we realized we were becoming accidental activists. We knew Esther alone had caused us to reevaluate our lives. Watching her walk side by side with our dogs, establishing herself as a member of our family, and growing into her larger-than-life personality has been all we've needed to see her for what she really is. She's really no different from a typical companion animal such as a cat or a dog; we just didn't know that until we knew her. And once that happened, we knew that if other people got to know her as we did, and saw that amazing smile for themselves, maybe they would start to see things differently too.

We acknowledged the crazy misconceptions around veganism, and rather than feed into them, we distanced ourselves and came at them from a different approach. No one wants to feel pressured. No one wants to be lectured, to be made to feel like a bad person. Our objective has never been to communicate, "We're vegan, and you must be vegan too!" We just wanted people to fall in love with a pig and start asking their own questions. And that's what has happened.

People started to feel like they were part of something. Small communities of fans have since created their own pages to discuss all kinds of stuff. They discuss everything from Esther's latest post to one another's favorite brand of plant-based milk, because they're trying to eliminate dairy from their diet. It's incredible, and it's all because of the sense of inclusivity we create on the page. We support people when they ask questions, and when they share a milestone such as giving up pork or beef as they work toward an "Esther-Approved" lifestyle. Even that term was created with the intention of being approachable; it's meant to open up a conversation, not to announce an edict.

Our message has always been one of kindness and positivity. Everything we've achieved has been because we approached it with kindness. Ninety-nine times out of a hundred upon hearing the term, someone will ask, "What does 'Esther-Approved' mean?" That doesn't happen when you just straight-out tell someone you're vegan, because people have preconceived notions about that. Some respond well, whereas others conjure up images of someone throwing flour at Kim Kardashian for wearing a fur coat and immediately view you as an extremist. (Even though she's the one wearing the skins of a few dozen animals that were likely electrocuted, and possibly skinned alive to avoid damaging the fur. Standing up for those animals doesn't sound so extreme when you look at it that way. Unfortunately, we aren't programmed to do that, thanks to the incredible marketing campaigns of the fashion industry. Similarly, we wouldn't stand up for a pig that was destined to become dinner until we got to know one.)

You can't demand that people do something that goes against what they've been taught their entire lives. You need to teach by example. You need to open up your life to how beneficial this lifestyle is for humans and animals alike. Through that, you will inspire people to change. We also fine-tuned the messaging on our social media pages, giving each a highly specific tone and direction. Esther's Kitchen has evolved into its very own community of people, tens of thousands of people just like us who are looking for ways to make their kitchen kinder and healthier.

We constantly provide new recipe ideas thanks to our amazing friend Chef Linda, who has cultivated a warm, welcoming place for people to learn how easy it is to start substituting products and making "Esther-Approved" meals at home. We've kept the focus on very familiar, family-friendly meals, because that's what the average person wants to eat. We left the fancy kale salads and quinoa burgers to the more advanced chefs.

The Esther's Army page has really taken on a life of its own. Its original purpose was to promote the crowdfunding campaign when we were trying to buy the farm. We knew the campaign would require some serious marketing, but we didn't want to dilute Esther's page with post after post about Indiegogo. Esther's Army let us tell people what they could do to help without our having to use our main pages as much. We could post memes and various calls to action that would help us spread the word much further than we ever could have on our own. By the end of the campaign, that page had more than ten thousand people on it, all working together to achieve a common goal. When the campaign ended, we had a huge network of people and nothing for them to do.

At the same time, we received a massive influx of messages to help find homes for animals all over the world. People knew we were opening a sanctuary, and they wanted to send us animals. We got messages from all over Canada, the United States, and even Europe, asking us to take in a pig here and a horse there. We wouldn't be able to help the vast majority of these animals, if for no other reason than geography. But we had our army, and they were situated all over the world, so we decided to put them to work again. Esther's Army has become a relocation/rehoming and advocacy powerhouse directly involved in the placement of almost 350 animals just in the past year, across dozens of countries. But we didn't stop there. We also use that page to do sanctuary spotlights, sharing information about various sanctuaries around the world and the people who run them.

Esther has made countless people sit up and take notice. Of course, they all want to meet her, but she's also making people pay attention to pigs in a way they hadn't before. We try to take advantage of their enthusiasm and direct them to a place where they can take their relationship with pigs to the next level: a sanctuary. Seeing a pig and getting to know one online is a wonderful way to open the door, but to really deepen that relationship, we think people need to actually interact with pigs, to see just how different each of their personalities is. Sanctuaries are invaluable for that, but they can't help if no one knows they're there.

We got lucky. We know that. Most sanctuaries do not get the exposure we've been able to create via Esther and our Happily Ever Esther Farm Sanctuary. But we think it's really important to remind her fans that they don't need to wait for a chance to visit Esther—there are other sanctuaries just like ours all over the place. I love getting a message from someone who says they did a Google search and found a farm sanctuary just an hour from their house in Texas. This lets us help not only the person who wants to create meaningful change, but also the sanctuary in their area—one that might be struggling to pay the feed bill or get volunteers to show up when needed.

I cannot even begin to fathom how someone could do this on their own, or even with a very small group of dedicated supporters. It takes a staggering amount of time, money, and energy to operate a sanctuary. We wouldn't survive if not for our volunteers.

The deeper into the world of animal rights we go, the more areas we see that need attention. But where do you draw the line to ensure you stay focused enough to be effective? We decided to stick as close as we could to pigs. For example, we flexed our advocacy muscles against pig-wrestling events—yet another thing we didn't know existed until we got involved in all things pig.

Pig wrestling is very common at county fairs and similar rural events. The organizers take a bunch of piglets or small adult pigs and throw them into a ring. Then they let a bunch of people chase them, wrestle them down, and drop them into buckets. It's incredibly cruel and unbelievably stressful for the pigs. Sometimes these events even use larger pigs, ones that require three or four people to pick them up. Pigs don't like to be picked up at the best of times, never mind being man-handled by strangers and dragged around by their legs. More often than not, the pigs get injured, sometimes mortally.

When we found out about these events, we immediately set out to stop them. We used Esther's Army to petition event organizers and speak to sponsors. Of course, we also implored community members not to attend. While we failed on many occasions, we did have some successes. We can directly attribute the cancellation of numerous pig-chase events to the work of Esther's Army. Everyone played a big role, but we have to give particular thanks to one special lady named Monica. She has become the general of our army, tirelessly devoting herself to making sure every animal that comes to our attention gets the best possible chance for a wonderful life. She personally attends some relocations, aids with transportation, or just lends moral support for the families involved. She also makes sure everything Esther's Army touches is handled the way Esther would do it: with kindness, understanding, and a smile on her face.

If Esther has taught us anything, it's that being kind to everyone you meet can have a bigger effect on your life than you could ever imagine. It sounds so lame, but every time someone asks how we made all this happen, the first thing we say is "Be kind to people." It's easy to get frustrated with any number of situations over the course of a day. Often the first thing people do is take to Facebook to air grievances.

We've been the subject of many vent posts from various activists, sometimes even sanctuary founders, who were upset about one thing or another we did or said. We learned very quickly that you can't please everyone, and complaining about it just drives a wedge between people.

There's enough negativity in the world, so make it your mission to be nothing but positive. Give people a break from the everyday downer news stories; make someone smile for a change. Stay focused on your goals, and believe that even when your closest friends think you're insane, anything is possible.

Our sanctuary has continued to grow, with new animals moving in on a regular basis. All of those visions we had in our heads are coming to fruition. The barn has been freshly painted in a traditional barn red with gleaming white trim. Our fences are up, and the stone walls are starting to look like walls again, not just big long piles of mossy rocks. We're settling into our new life, and Esther couldn't be happier we followed her lead.

I don't know about Derek, but I still pinch myself more than once a day to make sure it's not a dream. As I sit here typing these final few words, Esther is sleeping soundly on her queen-size mattress in the sunroom beside the table where I work, and there's a thirty-pound turkey named Cornelius standing behind me, demanding my attention. Just a typical day in our magical life, a life made possible thanks to a wonder pig named Esther, and a smile that's changing the world.

ESTHER-APPROVED RECIPES

Raspberry Overnight Oats
Fried Eggz and Toast
Thick Black Pepper–Maple, Smoked, Rice-Paper Bacon
Creamy Tomato Soup
Grilled Turky and Cheeze Sandwich
Esther's Pulled Jackfruit Carnitas
Wonder Scrapple
The Derek Burger
Steve's Garlic Parm Fries
Esther's Cashew Parmesan Cheeze
Esther's Macaroni and Cheeze with White Cheddar–
   Style Cheeze Sauce
Provolone Dolce–Style Cheeze
Mango Piña Colada
Chocolate Wine Cake

RASPBERRY OVERNIGHT OATS

Our Raspberry Overnight Oats are an easy and delicious breakfast or snack. They are very simple to make and save you time preparing breakfast the next morning. Enjoy your Raspberry Overnight Oats cold or warmed with a cup of coffee or tea at home. Eating on the run? Pop the jar and a spoon into your bag and off you go! This recipe is also a fun activity for children. These overnight oats are perfect to serve the next morning for children's sleepovers and guests. This recipe can be made the night before you need them and stored in the refrigerator for an additional 2 days.

Cuisine: Esther-Approved breakfast, gluten-free
Prep Time: 15 minutes
Refrigeration Time: Overnight
Yield: 4 servings (in 2-cup mason jars)

Ingredients

4 (2-cup) glass mason jars with seals and lids
2⅔ cups rolled oats
4 tablespoons chia seeds
4 tablespoons coconut palm sugar
8 teaspoons raspberry preserves
4 cups unsweetened almond milk
1 cup sliced almonds
1 cup fresh raspberries

Method

Layer the following ingredients, in this order, in each mason jar: ⅔ cup rolled oats, 1 tablespoon chia seeds, 1 tablespoon coconut palm sugar, 2 teaspoons raspberry preserves, 1 cup unsweetened almond milk, ¼ cup sliced almonds, ¼ cup fresh raspberries.

Place the seals on the jars and tighten the lids. Place the jars in the refrigerator overnight.

Serve the overnight oats with spoons.

Notes

Use certified gluten-free rolled oats for a gluten-free option. The coconut palm sugar may be replaced with maple syrup or vegan light brown sugar.

FRIED EGGZ AND TOAST

Now you can enjoy an Esther-Approved fried egg that is cholesterol-free and plant-based! Our Fried Eggz even have a savory "yolk." You will have extra "yolk" left over if you want to make your Fried Eggz runny after frying. For a big breakfast, serve two Fried Eggz with our Wonder Scrapple; Thick Black Pepper–Maple, Smoked, Rice-Paper Bacon; toast; orange juice; and coffee.

Cuisine: Esther-Approved breakfast, egg-free, gluten-free (Eggz only)
Prep Time: 15 minutes
Cook Time: 5 minutes per Eggz
Yield: 4 Fried Eggz

Center "Yolk" Ingredients

Makes 10 teaspoons
2 tablespoons nutritional yeast
1 teaspoon extra-virgin olive oil
6 teaspoons warm water
½ teaspoon kala namak salt
¼ teaspoon ground turmeric
2 teaspoons tapioca flour

Place the Center "Yolk" ingredients in a small bowl. Whisk with a fork until smooth. Set aside.

White Fried Eggz Ingredients

1 cup organic silken tofu
¼ teaspoon kala namak salt
¼ teaspoon onion powder
¼ cup tapioca flour
Vegan butter
Salt and pepper

Method

Combine the White Fried Eggz ingredients in a food processor or blender. Process until smooth. Place this batter in a 1-cup glass measure. Pour ¼ cup of the batter into a ¼-cup metal measure. Set aside. Heat a nonstick sauté pan or griddle to medium-high heat.

Spread 1 teaspoon vegan butter on the nonstick sauté pan or griddle for each Fried Eggz. The Eggz need oil to properly fry.

Pour ¼ cup of the White Fried Eggz batter for each egg, leaving room between the Eggz for the batter to slightly spread in a circle or oval shape on the skillet. Immediately create a 1-inch well in the center of each Eggz white, until the bottom of the pan is visible. Pour 1 teaspoon Eggz Yolk in the center of each White Fried Eggz round. Put the bread in the toaster at this stage.

Fry the first side for 3 minutes or until the surface of the Eggz is no longer moving. Flip the Eggz over. Fry this side for 2 minutes. The edges will bubble and crisp like a traditional fried egg. If the Eggz are undercooked, the texture will be chewy due to the tapioca starch. Flip the Eggz over and onto the serving plates so the Eggz Yolk is up. Pour additional Eggz Yolk onto the center if desired. Serve with toast and vegan butter. Add salt and pepper to taste.

Notes

Use a gluten-free bread for a gluten-free option. These Fried Eggz contain soy. Tapioca flour and kala namak salt can be purchased online if not available locally. Kala namak salt adds an eggy, sulfur taste to recipes.

THICK BLACK PEPPER–MAPLE, SMOKED, RICE-PAPER BACON

Rice-paper bacon rocks! This is a delicious, crispy bacon substitute that is peppery, smoky, and salty! It has all the classic flavors of a meat-based bacon but without the cholesterol. Serve it on your next Esther-Approved BLT sandwich, top avocado toast with it, or enjoy it with a chickpea or tofu breakfast scramble. Or just snack on it. Rice-paper sheets can be found in the international and Asian foods sections in your grocery store. They are also available online. The rice-paper bacon will stay crispy for up to 2 days if stored in a sealed container on the counter.

Cuisine: Esther-Approved bacon alternative, gluten-free
Prep Time: 30 minutes
Cook Time: 8 minutes
Yield: 20 (2-inch-wide) bacon strips

Ingredients

- 10 (8½-inch) dry, round rice-paper sheets (spring roll wrappers)
- 2 tablespoons canola or other neutral-flavor oil
- 2 tablespoons nutritional yeast
- 3 tablespoons soy sauce or tamari
- 2 teaspoons garlic powder
- 2 teaspoons smoked paprika
- 3 tablespoons maple syrup
- 1½ teaspoons freshly ground black pepper
- ½ teaspoon salt

Method

Line 2 baking sheets with parchment paper.

Preheat the oven to 400 degrees F.

Stack 2 rice-paper sheets together and hold them in place with one hand. With the other hand, cut the sheets into strips 2 inches wide, keeping matching pairs of strips together. Lay the matching strips out on your dry workspace. Do not stack them. Trim off the top and bottom of the matching strips and shape them into a rectangle to resemble bacon strips. Repeat the above steps with the remaining rice-paper sheets. (Don't worry if some of the strips break in half. You'll have a chance to mend them later.)

Combine the canola oil, nutritional yeast, soy sauce or tamari, garlic powder, smoked paprika, maple syrup, freshly ground black pepper, and salt in a small mixing bowl to make the sauce. Whisk until the ingredients are combined. Set aside.

Add warm water to a shallow bowl.

Holding 2 matching rice-paper strips together, dip them into the warm water quickly. Immediately run the combined strip between your forefinger and middle finger to remove excess water. If any of the strips broke during cutting, they can easily be mended by sticking them together with your fingers once they are dipped into the water.

Place the moistened strip on the parchment paper. Repeat this step with the remaining pairs of rice-paper strips, ensuring that the moistened strips do not touch each other on the parchment paper.

Whisk the sauce again. Lightly dip a pastry brush into the sauce. Evenly brush the sauce on the moistened rice-paper strips, lightly dipping your pastry brush into the sauce for each strip.

Turn the strips over on the parchment paper. Wash and dry your hands after turning all of the strips. Brush the remaining sauce onto this side of the strips.

Bake the rice-paper bacon for 8 minutes. Keep an eye on it after 7 minutes, as the strips can begin to burn on the edges. After 8 minutes, remove the rice-paper bacon strips from the oven. The baked strips will feel slightly soft but will crisp up once they cool.

Store the leftover rice-paper bacon in an airtight container. It will keep for 2 days.

CREAMY TOMATO SOUP

Coconut milk creates an amazing, smooth base for this Creamy Tomato Soup. Coconut milk is a great substitute for dairy cream–based soups. The easily sourced ingredients in this soup are pantry staples. Enjoy a Grilled Turky and Cheeze Sandwich with your soup.

Cuisine: Esther-Approved soup, dairy-free, gluten-free
Prep Time: 30 minutes
Yield: 4 bowls (5½ cups)

Ingredients

1 tablespoon extra-virgin olive oil
1 small yellow onion, diced
3 whole garlic cloves
2 teaspoons Italian seasoning
1 teaspoon pink Himalayan salt
1 teaspoon vegan granulated cane sugar
¼ teaspoon freshly ground black pepper
¼ teaspoon crushed red pepper flakes
1 (28-ounce) can plum tomatoes
1 (13.5-fluid-ounce) can full-fat coconut milk

Method

Heat the olive oil in a 2-quart stockpot over medium-high heat and sauté the onion and garlic until the onion is translucent, about 3 minutes.

Add the remaining ingredients to the same stockpot. Bring the soup to a boil. Stir and turn off the heat.

Purée the soup with a handheld immersion blender. Or ladle the soup into a blender pitcher. Blend on high until smooth. Release the lid slowly to allow steam to escape before pouring the soup into individual bowls. Serve.

GRILLED TURKY AND CHEEZE SANDWICH

Esther-Approved meatless deli slices are becoming more widely available in grocery stores. If they are not in your grocery store, ask the store manager to bring them in. The flavors and textures of these meatless products are spot-on! Tofurky Oven-Roasted Deli Slices are featured in our Grilled Turky and Cheeze Sandwich. Five of the Oven-Roasted Deli Slices offer 13 grams of plant protein! Another company that we love is Field Roast. Chao Creamy Original Slices by Field Roast taste very much like classic American cheese slices. On a side note, Field Roast also makes amazing sausages. Their sausages taste out of this world. Give them a try!

Cuisine: Esther-Approved sandwich
Prep Time: 15 minutes
Yield: 1 sandwich

Ingredients

3 slices Field Roast Chao Creamy Original cheese
2 slices Esther-Approved bread
5 Tofurky Deli Slices, Oven Roasted
Vegan butter

Method

Place the Chao cheese slices on 1 piece of bread. Place the Tofurky slices on top of the Chao cheese. Put the second slice of bread on top of the cheese to close the sandwich.

Spread vegan butter on the top piece of bread. Place this side down on a panini press or skillet. Spread vegan butter on the top piece of bread. If using a panini press, close it and grill the sandwich for 5 minutes on medium heat. If using a skillet, toast each side of the sandwich for 5 minutes over medium heat.

Slice in half and serve with Creamy Tomato Soup.

ESTHER'S PULLED JACKFRUIT CARNITAS

Pulled Jackfruit Carnitas is a recipe that's dear to our hearts because it's an Esther-Approved alternative to pork. "Carnitas" means "little meat." Our Pulled Jackfruit Carnitas recipe is a whole new delicious flavor experience in Esther-Approved cuisine. We hope you give Esther's recipe a try. It's an amazing base that you can launch into new recipes. Enjoy Esther's Pulled Jackfruit Carnitas on nachos, in tacos, on avocado toasts, and in tofu or chickpea scrambles. Canned, brined jackfruit is available in Asian and international grocery stores. This is also a kid-friendly recipe. Kids can help with the marinade step and squeeze the bag.

Cuisine: Esther-Approved meat alternative, gluten-free
Prep Time: 2 hours, 15 minutes
Bake Time: 20 minutes
Yield: 4 portions

Main Ingredient

1 (20-ounce) can jackfruit in brine, drained and unrinsed

Barbecue Marinade Ingredients

  1 teaspoon smoked paprika
  1 teaspoon chili powder
  1 teaspoon onion powder
  1 teaspoon garlic powder
  ½ teaspoon freshly ground black pepper
  ⅛ teaspoon ground cumin
  1 tablespoon tamari
  1 tablespoon maple syrup
  2 teaspoons ketchup
  1 tablespoon safflower, canola, or melted coconut oil
  Salt and pepper

Method

Place the jackfruit on a cutting board. Cut off the hard triangular core tip where it meets the upper stringy section. Chop the core into smaller pieces. Remove and discard the seeds from the stringy section of the jackfruit. Slice the stringy section in half. You will shred this later after the jackfruit bakes or fries.

Combine the Barbecue Marinade ingredients in a 1-quart sealable plastic bag. Add the jackfruit to the marinade bag. Seal the bag and hold the bag with both hands. Massage the bag to distribute the marinade evenly into the jackfruit. Set aside to marinate for 2 hours. Massage the bag a few times during the 2 hours.

Preheat the oven to 375 degrees F.

Spray an 8x8-inch baking dish with cooking spray. Pour the marinated jackfruit into the baking dish in a single layer. Bake for 20 minutes uncovered. Remove the dish from the oven. Use 2 forks to shred the jackfruit. Add salt and pepper to taste. Serve.

Notes

The jackfruit can be sautéed rather than baked. For this option, heat a sauté pan over medium-high heat. Add 1 tablespoon extra-virgin olive oil to the pan. Sauté the marinated jackfruit for 10 minutes, turning frequently. Use 2 forks to shred the jackfruit. Serve.

Soy sauce or Bragg Liquid Aminos may be substituted for tamari. Check the labels for any gluten allergens.

WONDER SCRAPPLE

Our Wonder Scrapple is Esther-Approved, meatless, and cholesterol-free! Enjoy these scrapple slices fried with a side of our Fried Eggz and Toast. They're also delicious served with maple syrup or ketchup. Enjoy our Wonder Scrapple as a sandwich too!

Cuisine: Esther-Approved meat alternative, gluten-free
Prep Time: 20 minutes
Cook Time: 10 minutes (5 minutes each side)
Refrigeration Time: Overnight
Yield: 9x5-inch loaf (nine ½-inch slices)

Seasoning Ingredients

1 tablespoon poultry seasoning
2 teaspoons ground sage
1 teaspoon garlic powder
1 teaspoon onion powder
1 teaspoon ground fennel seed
1 teaspoon freshly ground black pepper
1 teaspoon sea salt
⅛ teaspoon cayenne pepper
⅛ teaspoon allspice
½ teaspoon celery seed
Salt and pepper

Main Ingredients

1 tablespoon extra-virgin olive oil

8 ounces baby portobello mushrooms (caps and stems), finely diced

2 tablespoons Bragg Liquid Aminos

3 cups plus ¼ cup hot water

1 cup yellow cornmeal

½ cup instant oats

All-purpose flour, for coating slices before frying

Vegan butter

Salt and pepper

Method

Spray a 9x5-inch loaf pan with cooking spray. Coat the bottom and sides of the pan; set aside.

Combine all of the seasoning ingredients in a small bowl. Set aside.

Warm the olive oil in a nonstick pan over medium heat and sauté the mushrooms for 5 minutes, stirring occasionally.

Stir in the liquid aminos, and then add the hot water, cornmeal, and instant oats. Turn up the heat to medium-high and bring to a simmer. Cook for 2 minutes, stirring constantly.

Lower the heat to medium-low and simmer, continuing to stir. After approximately 8 minutes, the mixture will begin to pull away from the pan when stirred. After 8 minutes, add the seasoning ingredients and cook for 1 additional minute, stirring constantly.

Pour the mixture into the loaf pan. Allow the Wonder Scrapple to sit on the counter for 1 hour. Then cover the Wonder Scrapple with aluminum foil and refrigerate it overnight.

The Wonder Scrapple can be unmolded if desired: Allow the Wonder Scrapple to rest on the counter for 10 minutes after removing it from the refrigerator. Run a knife along the edges of the Wonder Scrapple. Jiggle the dish. Flip the dish onto a cutting board.

Slice each piece into ½-inch slices as you need them. Lightly coat each side with all-purpose flour. Tap off the excess flour. Heat a large nonstick sauté pan over medium heat. Add vegan butter to coat the bottom of the pan. Fry each side of the Wonder Scrapple for 5 minutes, flipping only once. Add salt and black pepper to taste before serving. When covered or wrapped tightly in plastic wrap or aluminum foil, the Wonder Scrapple will keep for 3 days in the refrigerator.

THE DEREK BURGER

The Derek Burger is named after Esther's dad Derek Walter. This juicy and rich meatless burger has the texture of ground meat from textured vegetable protein! Enjoy the Derek Burger paired with Steve's Garlic Parm Fries and a lager beer. Our Thick Black Pepper–Maple, Smoked, Rice-Paper Bacon and Provolone Dolce–Style Cheeze are featured along with bottled Esther-Approved barbecue sauce!

Cuisine: Esther-Approved burger (meatless)
Prep Time: 35 minutes
Refrigeration Time: 1 hour
Cooking Time: 8 minutes (4 minutes per side)
Yield: 7 burgers

Ingredients

2 cups textured vegetable protein (TVP)

½ cup rolled oats

8 ounces baby portobello mushrooms, stemmed and quartered

3¼ cups boiling water

1½ teaspoons onion powder

1 teaspoon garlic powder

¼ teaspoon freshly ground black pepper

½ teaspoon sea salt

1½ teaspoons smoked paprika

¼ cup Esther-Approved barbecue sauce

¼ cup nutritional yeast

¼ cup plus 1 tablespoon vital wheat gluten flour

Method

Place the TVP in a large mixing bowl. Set aside.

Combine the rolled oats, mushrooms, boiling water, onion powder, garlic powder, freshly ground black pepper, sea salt, smoked paprika, barbecue sauce, and nutritional yeast in a blender. Process until smooth.

Pour the blender contents over the TVP. Stir with a silicone spatula until all the ingredients are combined. Set aside for 15 minutes to allow the TVP to rehydrate.

Add the vital wheat gluten flour to the rehydrated TVP mixture. Stir with a silicone spatula for 1 minute.

Form the Derek Burgers into ½-cup-measured patties with your hands. Line a small baking tray with waxed paper. Place the Derek Burgers on the paper. Refrigerate the burgers for 1 hour so they will set up.

Heat the grill to medium. Generously spray the grill with cooking spray. Place the burgers on the grill. Spray the tops of the burgers with cooking spray. Grill each burger for 4 minutes on each side. The Derek Burgers will darken as they grill. Serve with Esther-Approved Cheeze, buns, and condiments.

Notes

The Derek Burgers, in uncooked patties, can be frozen for up to 1 month. This recipe contains soy and gluten.

STEVE'S GARLIC PARM FRIES

Steve's Garlic Parm Fries were inspired by amazing garlicky fries Steve once had at a restaurant. Esther's Cashew Parmesan Cheeze is featured in this recipe and is a fridge staple in Esther's Kitchen. Serve Steve's Garlic Parm Fries with ketchup and additional salt to taste. Steve's Garlic Parm Fries pair well with the Derek Burger.

Cuisine: Esther-Approved side, dairy-free, gluten-free
Prep Time: 10 minutes
Bake Time: 18–20 minutes
Yield: 1 serving

Ingredients

1 large russet potato, sliced into french fry pieces
½ teaspoon dried parsley
1 large garlic clove, minced
2 tablespoons Esther's Cashew Parmesan Cheeze (see recipe on page 216)

Method

Preheat the oven to 400 degrees F. Line a baking tray with parchment paper. Spray the paper with cooking spray.

Lay the potato slices on the parchment paper and spray them with cooking spray. Set aside.

In a small bowl, combine the parsley, garlic, and Cashew Parmesan Cheeze. Stir to combine.

Sprinkle the mixture over each potato slice. Bake the fries for 18 to 20 minutes, turning the fries once after 10 minutes. Serve.

ESTHER'S CASHEW PARMESAN CHEEZE

Esther's Cashew Parmesan Cheeze may become a refrigerator staple once you try it. Sprinkle Esther's Cashew Parmesan Cheeze on pasta, soups, avocado toast, salads, and dairy-free lasagna and pizza. This dairy-free and gluten-free topping is great for those with allergies. If there is a cashew allergy, the cashews can be replaced with the same measurement of raw sunflower seeds.

Cuisine: Esther-Approved nut Cheeze, dairy-free, gluten-free
Prep Time: 10 minutes
Yield: 1¼ cups

Ingredients

1 cup unsalted raw cashews
4 tablespoons nutritional yeast
½ teaspoon garlic powder
1 teaspoon sea salt or pink Himalayan salt

Method

Combine all ingredients in a food processor or blender.
Pulse the mixture to a parmesan cheese texture.
Refrigerate Esther's Cashew Parmesan Cheeze in a sealed jar or shaker jar. It will keep for up to 2 months.
Sprinkle on foods wherever you would use parmesan cheese. It's delicious on pasta, salads, soups, raw and cooked veggies, lasagna, pizza, sandwiches, and popcorn.

ESTHER'S MACARONI AND CHEEZE WITH WHITE CHEDDAR–STYLE CHEEZE SAUCE

Esther's Macaroni and Cheeze with White Cheddar–Style Cheeze Sauce is the ultimate comfort food! This rich and creamy macaroni and Cheeze is made without dairy cheese! The White-Cheddar–Style Cheeze Sauce is made with ingredients that you may currently have in your pantry. Tapioca flour and miso paste are the ingredients you might need from the store. The tapioca flour creates a stretchy Cheeze sauce. Tapioca flour can be found in the Asian food or alternative flours section in grocery stores. Tapioca flour is also available online. There are a few varieties of miso paste. Miso may contain gluten. Please check the ingredients label. Use your favorite gluten-free pasta of choice if you desire a gluten-free macaroni and Cheeze.

Cuisine: Esther-Approved, dairy-free, gluten-free (if using gluten-free macaroni, gluten-free white miso paste, and gluten-free panko bread crumbs)
Prep Time: 40 minutes
Bake Time: 15 minutes
Yield: 8 servings

Ingredients

½ teaspoon sea salt
1 pound elbow macaroni

White Cheddar–Style Cheeze Sauce Ingredients

1 (13.5-fluid-ounce) can full-fat coconut milk
2 cups unsweetened almond milk
1 teaspoon garlic powder
1 teaspoon onion powder
2 tablespoons tapioca flour
1 tablespoon extra-virgin olive oil
1½ teaspoons sea salt
¼ cup white miso paste
1 cup instant potato flakes
⅛ teaspoon cayenne pepper

Topping Ingredient

1 cup panko bread crumbs

Method

Fill a large pot with 6 quarts of water and add the sea salt. Bring to a boil over high heat. Add the macaroni and cook uncovered until al dente, about 8 minutes. Stir occasionally while the macaroni is cooking to prevent sticking. Drain the macaroni and set aside.

Combine the White Cheddar–Style Cheeze Sauce ingredients in a blender. Process on high until smooth.

Preheat the oven to 350 degrees F. Spray a 9x13-inch baking dish with cooking spray. Set aside.

Pour the blended Cheeze sauce into a large sauté pan. Turn the burner to medium-high. Stir the sauce constantly and scrape the sides of the pan with a silicone spatula for the duration of the cooking time. Bring the sauce to a simmer. Lower the heat to medium. Cook for 12 minutes or until slightly thickened.

Add the macaroni to the baking dish. Pour the White Cheddar–Style Cheeze Sauce over the macaroni. Stir to combine. Sprinkle the panko bread crumbs on top. Bake uncovered for 15 minutes. Serve warm.

PROVOLONE DOLCE–STYLE CHEEZE

Traditional provolone dolce cheese is naturally smoked and ages for 2 to 3 months. It's semi-soft and smooth with a mild, sweet taste. This cheese originated in southern Italy. Our Esther-Approved, dairy-free version is similar to the traditional cheese. Agar-agar is used to firm up our Provolone Dolce–Style Cheeze. We find that when coconut milk is mixed with almond milk, they impart a flavor similar to that of dairy milk. The white miso paste adds a sweet, mild umami flavor to this Cheeze. The unmolding of the Cheeze works best if using a bowl with flared sides. The Cheeze can be sliced after 2 hours of refrigeration. It can be grated once it has refrigerated overnight. Enjoy our Provolone Dolce–Style Cheeze with crackers or on the Derek Burger or other entrées.

Cuisine: Esther-Approved Cheeze, dairy-free, gluten-free
Prep Time: 25 minutes
1st Refrigeration Time: 35 minutes to unmold
2nd Refrigeration Time: 2 hours or overnight for firmest
   Cheeze
Yield: 13.8 ounces

Ingredients

6 tablespoons agar-agar flakes
¼ cup boiling water
½ cup unsalted raw cashews, ground into flour in a food
   processor or blender
1 cup full-fat coconut milk
½ cup unsweetened almond milk
¼ cup instant potato flakes
1 tablespoon fresh lemon juice
1 tablespoon extra-virgin olive oil
1 tablespoon white miso paste
½ teaspoon liquid smoke
1½ teaspoons sea salt
Pinch ground turmeric
½ teaspoon tahini
1 tablespoon tapioca flour

Method

Place the agar-agar flakes in a small glass measuring cup. Pour the ¼ cup boiling water over the agar-agar flakes. Stir with a butter knife until all the flakes are combined with the water. Scrape the excess gel off the knife and put it back into the mixture. Set aside on the counter for 10 minutes to allow the flakes to set up.

Combine the remaining ingredients in a blender. Once the agar-agar mixture has set up, add it to the blender. Process on high until smooth.

Pour the Cheeze mixture into an 11-inch sauté pan on the stove. Scrape out any remaining mixture with a silicone spatula and add it to the pan. Cook over medium heat, constantly stirring the Cheeze and scraping the sides of the pan, for 7 minutes. The Cheeze eventually will thicken and pull away from the pan when the spatula moves through it. At that point, immediately pour the Cheeze into an ungreased glass or plastic bowl. Quickly smooth out the top with the spatula. Place the Cheeze in the refrigerator for 35 minutes. Invert the bowl onto a small plate to unmold the Cheeze. Gently run your finger over the Cheeze surface to smooth it if necessary. Cover the Cheeze with plastic wrap and refrigerate for an additional 2 hours. For the firmest Cheeze, refrigerate overnight.

Mango Piña Colada

Our Mango Piña Colada cocktail was inspired by Esther's love of mangoes and the fabulous piña coladas we had on the first Esther Cruise! Each cocktail has 2 ounces of light rum. Please drink responsib-pig-ly.

Cuisine: Esther-Approved cocktail, dairy-free, gluten-free
Prep Time: 10 minutes
Yield: 4 glasses

Piña Colada Ingredients

3 cups frozen diced pineapple
1 (13.5-fluid-ounce) can full-fat coconut milk
½ cup light rum
1 cup ice

Mango Layer Ingredients

1 cup frozen diced pineapple
2 cups frozen diced mango
½ cup light rum

Garnish Ingredients

4 slices fresh mango, sliced from one side of a ripe mango
4 pieces diced fresh pineapple

Method

Combine the Piña Colada ingredients in a blender pitcher. Process until smooth. Pour the piña colada evenly into 4 glasses.

Using the same pitcher with leftover Piña Colada ingredients in it, combine the Mango Layer ingredients in the pitcher. Blend until smooth. Pour the mango layer over the piña colada layer.

Garnish the top of each drink with a slice of fresh mango. Add a piece of fresh pineapple next to each mango slice.

CHOCOLATE WINE CAKE

Serve our Chocolate Wine Cake at your next soirée. This deep, rich, and super-moist chocolate cake is delicious served with your favorite Esther-Approved red wine. This recipe came about one day while making a chocolate cake and drinking wine. Chocolate and red wine pair nicely together, so we added ½ cup of red wine to the cake batter. We baked the cake and needed a glaze for it. There was still some wine left, so we made a quick wine glaze and brushed it on the warm cake. We sliced the warm Chocolate Wine Cake and enjoyed it with a glass of wine from a new bottle, and a party started! Check out Barnivore.com for Esther-Approved wines.

Cuisine: Esther-Approved dessert
Prep Time: 30 minutes
Bake Time: 50 minutes
Yield: 10 slices

Cake Ingredients

½ cup chopped walnuts
1 tablespoon flax meal
3 tablespoons warm water
1 cup all-purpose flour
½ cup unsweetened cocoa powder
1 teaspoon sea salt
½ cup vegan light brown sugar
¾ cup vegan granulated sugar
¼ cup vegan butter, melted
½ cup dairy-free, plain yogurt
1 teaspoon baking powder
½ teaspoon baking soda
2 teaspoons apple cider vinegar
½ cup vegan red wine
1 teaspoon vanilla extract

Wine Glaze Ingredients

2 tablespoons vegan butter
⅓ cup vegan granulated sugar
2 tablespoons warm water
¼ cup vegan red wine

Method

Preheat the oven to 350 degrees F.

Spray the bottom and sides of a 9x5-inch loaf pan with cooking spray. Add the walnuts to the bottom of the loaf pan. Set aside.

In a small bowl, combine the flax meal and water. Swirl in the bowl and set aside for 10 minutes to let the mixture gel up.

In a large bowl, combine the all-purpose flour, unsweetened cocoa powder, sea salt, vegan light brown sugar, and vegan granulated sugar. Stir to combine and break up any lumps. Add the remaining cake ingredients. Stir the batter with a silicone spatula until smooth.

Pour the cake batter over the chopped walnuts. Scrape out all of the batter into the pan. Bake the cake for 50 minutes or until a toothpick inserted into the middle comes out clean.

Place the hot cake, still in the pan, on a cooling rack for 10 minutes. Place aluminum foil under the cooling rack. Turn the cake out of the loaf pan and onto the cooling rack. While the cake is cooling for another 10 minutes, make the Wine Glaze.

In a nonstick, 2-quart saucepan, combine the vegan butter, vegan granulated sugar, and the water. Stir and bring this to a boil over medium-high heat. Stir the glaze constantly for 5 minutes. The top will begin to foam. At 5 minutes, remove the pan from the heat. Immediately stir in the red wine. Continue to stir until the glaze is smooth.

Brush the hot wine glaze over the top and sides of the cake. Continue to brush until all of the wine glaze has been used.

Allow the cake to further cool for 1 hour. Slice and serve. Or wrap the cooled cake in waxed paper and foil, then refrigerate until ready to serve. This cake can be made up to one day in advance of serving.

ACKNOWLEDGMENTS

Thanks to:

Our parents and siblings. Your unwavering love and support mean the world to both of us. No matter how wild it may seem, having family by our side on this amazing adventure is everything.

Our amazing circle of friends. For putting up with us and being there when we need someone to talk to. We don't know how we got so lucky, or what we would do without you.

Dr. David Kirkham and the entire staff of Cheltenham Veterinary Centre and the Ontario Veterinary College at the University of Guelph. Where do we even begin? Thank you doesn't seem like enough. Esther has the best medical team on earth, and you have given us peace of mind in unfathomably scary situations. Thank you for putting up with us and for taking such incredible care of our baby girl.

Caprice Crane. Your sense of humor is unparalleled. We won the lottery when we connected with you, and we will forever be grateful for your help in turning our words into something magical.

Erica Silverman. Our agent, navigator, and friend. You're another person we will forever wonder how we got lucky enough to know.

Katherine Stopa. Our editor, and one of the biggest reasons this book exists. Thank you for being such an amazing cheerleader, and for making sure our story was told. We're so thankful to have you in our corner. Team Esther wouldn't be the same without you.

And to the countless people we have met on this incredible journey. Your messages and comments give us all the motivation we could ever need. No matter how hard it gets, you inspire us to work harder.

This book would not have been possible if it were not for each and every one of you.

ABOUT THE AUTHORS

It has been a whirlwind few years for *New York Times* best-selling authors **Steve Jenkins** and **Derek Walter**. Accumulating close to two million followers from all over the world in just a few short years, they have very quickly become two of the world's most well-known and successful animal activists. In 2014, Steve and Derek founded the Happily Ever Esther Farm Sanctuary in Campbellville, Ontario, where they continue to rescue and rehabilitate abandoned and abused farmed animals.

Caprice Crane is an award-winning, *New York Times* best-selling five-time novelist, screenwriter, and television writer with her finger on the pulse of pop culture. Caprice's humor and satirical observations have earned her the distinction of being one of the *Huffington Post*'s "50 Funny People You Should Be Following on Twitter." Her debut novel *Stupid and Contagious* (published in fourteen countries) and her equally internationally bestselling *Forget About It* won the RT Reviews Choice Award in 2006 and 2007, respectively. She has since published three more novels to critical acclaim and, with the publication of the first Esther book, *Esther the Wonder Pig*, won a 2016 Nautilus Book Award.